STOCKS, STRATEGIES & COMMON SENSE

BART DILIDDO, PhD

EDITOR AND FOUNDER OF THE VECTORVEST ADVISORY

Second Edition

HSC PUBLISHERS

Copyright ©1995-2003 by Dr. Bart DiLiddo, PhD.

VectorVest
330-668-2814
P.O. Box 577, Bath Ohio 44210-0577

Published in association with HSC Publishing, a division of Homeschool Computer, P.O. Box 3, Kanona, New York 14856-0003

All rights reserved. No part of this publication may be reproduced, stored in a retrieval system or transmitted in any form by any means, electronic, mechanical, photocopy, recording or otherwise, without the prior permission of the publisher, except as provided by USA copyright law.

Cover Design: Richard A. Fairchild II

First Printing, 1995
Second Printing, 1996
Revised and expanded, Third Printing, June 1997
Fourth Printing, April 1998
Fifth Printing, September 1998
Sixth Printing, May 1999
Seventh Printing, April 2000
Eighth Printing, February 2001
Ninth Printing, June 2001
Tenth Printing, March 2002
Eleventh Printing, November 2003
Twelfth Printing, December 2003

Printed in the United States of America

STOCKS, STRATEGIES & COMMON SENSE

Table of Contents

The Five Greatest Stock Market Myths

Myth #1.
PRICE TO EARNINGS RATIOS TELL YOU WHETHER STOCKS ARE CHEAP OR EXPENSIVE.

P/E ratios are easy to find. Just about every newspaper, magazine and stock report publishes P/E ratios. Everybody seems to talk about them when discussing stocks. So P/E ratios must be a great way to compare stocks.

Right? Wrong!

If you were told that Fly-By-Nite Industries had a P/E of 7, and Fantastic Plastics Inc. had a P/E of 14, would you buy Fly-By-Nite Industries instead of Fantastic Plastics Inc.? You might, but you wouldn't be comfortable making that decision. Why? Because you need more information. You'd like to know a whole lot of things before you decide which stock to buy. One of the most important things you'd like to know is the worth of each stock based upon its earnings, profitability and other key financial data. In other words, you'd like to have a sense of the stock's intrinsic value. P/E ratios don't say anything about a stock's value!

What investors need is a Value to Price ratio. With a Value to Price ratio, investors would know immediately whether a stock was cheap, expensive or fairly priced. But this means we have to have a way of computing value. Of course there are theories and formulas for computing intrinsic value. But they are complex, and some sophisticated investors even say they are unfathomable. Consequently, most investors, even the Pros, don't begin to look at stock's intrinsic value! They resort to trivial devices like comparing P/E ratios.

Myth #2.
YOU MUST ASSUME HIGH RISKS TO
MAKE GOOD MONEY IN THE STOCK MARKET.

A woman recently said to me, "I'm just scared to death of stocks. I can't afford to lose my hard earned money." The perception of high risk in stock investing is not totally without merit. Many investors have lost substantial sums of money in the market. Visions of investors jumping out of windows back in 1929 are graphic reminders of the risk inherent in stock investing.

Recent events on the market...the Great Crash of '87, the Friday the 13th Mini-meltdown, the ills of Program Trading, insider trading, the Mercury Financial and Bre-X scandals, have also contributed to the casino image associated with stock investing. This is very unfortunate because stock investing is one of the best ways the average person has of accumulating substantial wealth. It just requires a few simple techniques and some discipline. In fact, it can be a lot safer than investing in real estate, collectibles, or your own business.

Here's how to make good money in stocks at low risk:

1. Buy stocks with consistent, predictable earnings growth.
2. Buy stocks with earnings growth rates equal to or greater than the sum of current inflation and interest rates.
3. Do not put more than 10% of your money into any single stock.
4. Do not own more than two stocks in the same industry.
5. Do not plunge into the market. Spread your investments over time.
6. Use Stop-Sell orders to limit risk.

Stocks with consistent, predictable earnings growth are the safest stocks you can buy. They represent the best managed companies in America. A stock portfolio with an average earnings growth rate of at least 14%/yr. has a high probability of doubling in five years. In twenty years it will have increased by 1,500 percent.

If you bought 10 stocks, and limited your loss on any single stock to 10% by using Stop-Sell orders, your total portfolio risk is only 10%. Your risk on any single stock is only 1% of your total portfolio. How many investments can you think of that have the upside potential of stocks with such limited risk exposure?

Myth #3.
BUY STOCKS ON THE WAY DOWN
AND SELL ON THE WAY UP.

There's an old adage that says the way to make money in the stock market is to buy low and to sell high. That, of course, is an irrefutable truth. The only problem is that many investors confuse this bit of conventional wisdom with the assumption that if the price of a stock is going down it is low, and if it is going up it is high. Consequently, they buy stocks on the way down and sell on the way up. There's hardly a worse thing an investor could do.

Stocks are bought on the expectation that they will go up. If a stock is going up in price, it is fulfilling that expectation. When the price is going down, it is denying that expectation. Therefore, it is logical to buy a stock when its price is going up. Moreover, one of the best times to buy a stock is when the price has broken above an old high. At this point there are no unhappy holders who are waiting to dump the stock. If the stock is fairly valued, there should be clear sailing ahead.

Myth #4.
STOCKS ARE A HEDGE AGAINST INFLATION.

For many years stockbrokers and mutual fund salesmen have been saying that stocks are a hedge against inflation. Well, they are and they aren't. It depends on how you look at it.

A true inflation hedge is one that goes up in value with higher inflation...like a house, or gold, or collectibles. But, the fact is, inflation is the stock market's number one enemy. When inflation goes up, interest rates go up and two things happen. For one thing, investors say, "Golly, I can make all that money on high interest rate bonds so why should I invest in stocks." So they take their money out of the stock market, and stock prices go down. The second thing that happens is that the cost of doing business goes up. So corporate earnings go down, and stock prices go down.

So why in the world would anybody say that stocks are a hedge against inflation? It's because they can make money in stocks faster than inflation will eat it up. All they have to do is invest in stocks which have earnings growth

7

rates higher than the sum of inflation and long-term interest rates. When they do that, the price of the stock will go up faster than inflation. And they will be whipping inflation by staying ahead of it.

Myth #5.
YOUNG PEOPLE CAN AFFORD
TO TAKE HIGH RISK.

Of all the myths in the market, this may be the cruelest and the most foolish. Everyone knows that the elderly are not supposed to take risks. They must be very conservative because their earnings power is limited. They can't afford to lose their money! Well, who decided that young people could afford to lose their money?

If any group needed to watch every penny, it's the young. They need money to start a family, buy a house, buy furniture, save for the future and on and on. Furthermore, young people usually are at the low end of the earnings scale. They have precious little disposable income.

Young people have an invaluable asset on their side, however. Time. They don't need to take risk. They can invest in tried and true companies that make money year in and year out. At 10%/year growth, their investments will double every seven years. By the time baby is off to college, that initial safe investment has increased by a factor of eight.

When you have time, you can afford patience. Patience pays off in the market.

How to Pick Stocks

Visit the business section of any decent library. You'll find shelves full of books on how to pick stocks. I've read most of them over the last thirty years, and some are pretty good. Most are not. It isn't easy, but sorting the good stuff from the not-so-good is absolutely necessary. Anyone who has read John Rothchild's *"A Fool and His Money,"* knows what I mean.

The biggest obstacle to finding a winning stock picking system is that no system works all the time. Even the great Peter Lynch picked bummers once in a while. Nevertheless, there are some simple, common sense rules that can improve anyone's stock picking skills regardless of the system they use. Here they are:

Rule I: Favor Undervalued Stocks. The first step in picking stocks is to favor stocks of companies that are making money, lots of money. Study stocks of companies with rapidly growing earnings, and choose stocks of companies which consistently make more money than they did the year before.

The question of price arises even if you do the above. Profitable, high growth stocks usually sell at very high prices. How high of a price is too high?

9

The only way to answer this question is to know what a stock is really worth. I answer this question by calculating a stock's value from its earnings growth rate, profitability and other fundamentals. My formulas for calculating value are described in Chapter 3 of this book, **"How to Value Stocks."** If a stock's Value is more than its Price, the stock is undervalued. It's a candidate for selection.

Undervalued stocks offer a higher probability of achieving gains, the potential for very large gains, and lower downside risk. In other words, undervalued stocks increase the odds of winning, increase the rewards for winning, and decrease the risk of losing compared to overvalued stocks. So, favor undervalued stocks.

Rule II: Favor Safe Stocks. Have you ever noticed that the prices of stocks like Coca Cola and McDonalds never seem to cause any excitement, yet go up year after year? Stocks like Chrysler are always in the news, and go up and down like a yo-yo. There's a very simple reason for this contrast. The former have track records of steady earnings performance while the latter has an erratic earnings record. Price volatility is a reflection of fear and uncertainty.

Price volatility and risk arise from many sources...rumors, political assassinations, earthquakes and so on. Shareholders with little confidence in their company tend to overreact to rumors and bad news. Consequently, the stock prices of companies with erratic earnings performance suffer more when unfortunate things happen. Stocks of companies with steady, predictable earnings can weather nearly any storm.

Obviously, there's less risk in holding stocks of financially stable companies. Consequently, I analyze the risk factors of stocks very carefully before buying. A discussion of how I assess risk is given in Chapter 7, **"Stock Safety: The Missing Link."**

The second key factor in picking stocks is to favor safe stocks.

Rule III: Favor Stocks with Rising Prices. The hardest thing for most investors to do is buy a stock while its price is rising. Most of us have been taught to wait for a stock to go down before buying it. The idea of buying stock at a lower price makes a lot of sense, but is fallacious.

First of all, you'll miss a lot of good opportunities. Really good stocks usually don't look back once they have started moving upward. Witness the hundreds of stocks that have doubled and tripled over the last few years with nary a downturn.

Even more importantly, you never know where the bottom is when buying a stock whose price is falling. Remember when IBM went from 175 7/8 to 37 5/8. Who'd of believed it? I did because VectorVest did not reflect IBM as being undervalued or safe as it was going down. However, when things started turning around and IBM's price started rising again, we gave it a buy signal.

Buying stocks on the way down lessens your chances of winning. Most of us dream of buying a stock as its low point and riding it to the moon. It's a great dream, but the chances of doing so are virtually nil. The low points on good stocks don't last long. You have to be very lucky to bag a bottom.

Picking stocks with rising prices not only obviates the above problems, but offers several advantages. First, a stock that is rising in price is already doing what you want it to do. (You don't have to break a rising stock of a bad habit.)

Buying stocks with rising prices does not preclude the idea of buying them right after they hit bottom. Bottom Fishing is a great sport and I discuss it in Chapter 15. You just have to know when the price trend has gone from down to up. I tell you how to know what a stock's price is doing in Chapter 9, **"Timing: The Ultimate Weapon."**

Finally, a stock that is hitting new highs, has essentially no overhead resistance. There are no unhappy buyers waiting to get their money back. I especially like to buy stocks hitting their very first 52 week high. These stocks have had plenty of time to consolidate, and are showing new signs of life.

It's fun to own stocks with rising prices. So pick stocks with rising prices.

Rule of Rules: Pick Safe, Undervalued Stocks with Rising Prices. That's easy to say, but how does one find safe, undervalued stocks rising in price? Try following these steps:

1. Look at the financial section of your local paper, the Wall Street Journal, Investors Business Daily, Barrons, the internet or whatever. Find the list of stocks that have just hit new 52 week highs. All of these stocks are definitely rising in price.
2. Rank all these stocks in ascending order of Price to Earnings ratio, i.e., P/E ratio. This may take some work, but low P/E ratio stocks of course, are undervalued.
3. Assess each stock for safety. Since the subject of safety is not touched upon in the papers, you'll have to turn to other sources. Take a look at Value Line for example, or Standard & Poor's Stock Guide.

4. Now put all the information together in a logical, quantitative, unemotional way. Pick the ones you think are the safest, most undervalued and rising in price the fastest.

Once you have prepared your list of stocks, check them out using VectorVest ProGraphics. VectorVest ProGraphics stock analysis and graphics software analyzes over 7,600 stocks every day for Value, Safety and Timing. It unifies these factors into a comprehensive indicator called VST-Vector. Stocks with the highest VST-Vector ratings have the best combinations of Value, Safety and Timing.

There's no need to spend hours and hours doing what a computer can do. You can obtain a complete, rank analysis of any list of stocks with VectorVest ProGraphics in just a few minutes. Our records show that stocks with the highest VST-Vector ratings outperform the market over the long-term.

This comes as no surprise. Common sense and simple logic dictate that picking safe, undervalued stocks rising in price should result in above average performance.

How To Value Stocks

"How do we know when irrational exuberance has unduly escalated asset values, which then become subject to unexpected and prolonged contractions as they have in Japan over the past decades?"

These words, spoken on the evening of December 5, 1996 by Dr. Alan Greenspan, Chairman of the Federal Reserve Board, unleashed a selling frenzy that ripped around the world. Prices plunged in Asia, Europe and England. The mighty Dow Jones Industrial Average fell 145 points the next morning in New York. It closed down 55.16 points for the day.

Indeed, how do we know when stock prices are too high? All serious investors are asking this question. Surely, the Wizards of Wall Street must have the answer. Why, then, was Dr. Greenspan, America's most powerful financial person, posing the question? Was he just sending a message, or does he really want to know if stock prices are too high?

Our guess is that Dr. Greenspan was sending a message, but our work on stock valuation over the last 19 years says he's wrong.

13

The theory of stock valuation is relatively simple, but it is terribly difficult to apply. It is described best by the classic "Dividend Discount Model" which is theoretically elegant, but not practical. Not only is it based upon a number of assumptions regarding dividend payments, growth rates and risk factors which usually amount to little more than guesswork, but it is mathematically unstable. The answers it gives are usually worthless. How can we get realistic valuations of stocks based upon facts rather than assumptions?

Let's examine the way the stock and bond markets work. They are driven by three powerful forces: earnings, interest rates and inflation, and they compete ferociously for investors' money. Investors pour money into stocks when corporate earnings go up, and the perception of value has increased. Money flows into bonds when interest rates go up, and investors receive higher yields. The converse is also true.

Money goes where money grows. Stock prices go up when corporate earnings go up, and go down when interest rates go up. Stock prices are also affected indirectly by inflation rates. Rising inflation rates drive interest rates up which, in turn, suck money out of the stock market and pull stock prices down. In summary:

Stock prices go up when:

1. Corporate earnings go up.
2. Interest rates go down, and
3. Inflation rates go down.

Given this scenario, how do investors decide where to put their money? Since investors are constantly seeking to maximize their returns they buy stocks when they think the total return would be more than that of buying bonds. In other words, the stock's price appreciation and dividend payout would be more than the compounded interest payments of bonds. They buy bonds when they think that bonds provide a higher return.

In the case of bonds, it's easy to know exactly what one would need to pay to receive a given return. Simply divide the annual interest payment by the interest yield. This is calculated as follows:

$$BP = 100*(IP/IY) \quad \text{Eq.}(1)$$

Where: BP = Bond Price in $/Share
                      IP = Annual Interest Payment in $
                      IY = Interest Yield in Percent

For example: The price of a bond paying an annual interest payment of $100 and yielding 8.0 percent would be $1,250.

$$BP = 100*(100/8.0) \qquad \text{Eq. (1)}$$
$$= 100*(12.5)$$
$$= \$1,250$$

With stocks, however, there is far less certainty regarding the returns one might receive. Even after a buyer and seller have negotiated a stock's price, neither party knows whether, when, or how long the stock will pay any dividends. Certainly, the potential for receiving dividends from a stock comes only from a company's earnings. So the place to start in assessing the price one should pay for a stock is from its earnings rate of return.

We can find a stock's earnings rate of return simply by looking at a stock's Price to Earnings ratio, i.e., P/E ratio. This common measure of stock valuation can be found in virtually any newspaper. The Earnings Yield for a stock may be obtained from its P/E ratio as follows:

$$EY = 100*[1/(P/E)] \qquad \text{Eq. (2)}$$

Where: EY = Earnings Yield in Percent
P = Stock Price in $/Share
E = Earnings Per Share in $/Share

For example: The Earnings Yield of a stock with a P/E ratio of 16 would be 6.25 percent.

$$EY = 100*[1/(16)] \qquad \text{Eq. (2)}$$
$$= 100*(0.0625)$$
$$= 6.25\%$$

As an aside, the average P/E ratio of 5,751 stocks in the VectorVest database as of January 3, 1997, was 16.4.

Since stocks are normally far riskier than AAA Corporate bonds, the least we should expect from a stock is that its Earnings Yield would be equal to the bond's Interest Yield. In other words:

Stock Earnings Yield = Bond Interest Yield
$$EY = IY \qquad \text{Eq. (3)}$$
or $\qquad 100*(E/P) = IY \qquad \text{Eq. (4)}$

We can determine the price we would be willing to pay for a stock from a bond's interest yield by simply re-arranging Eq. (4). Thus:

$$P = 100*(E/IY) \qquad \text{Eq. (5)}$$

If we were to use the AAA Corporate Bond rate as standard measure of return, we would get an estimate of the inherent Value of a stock by simply dividing the stock's annual earnings per share by the current AAA Corporate Bond rate.

$$V = 100*(E/I) \qquad \text{Eq. (6)}$$

Where: V = Value of a Stock in $/share
               I = AAA Corp. Bond Rate in percent

This equation is called our "Quick Value Estimate." Let's see what the "Quick Value Estimate" of McDonalds Corp. would be as of January 3, 1997. VectorVest's estimate of McDonalds' leading 12 month earnings per share is $2.53. The long term AAA Corporate Bond rate was 7.60 percent. Inserting these figures into Eq. (6) gives us:

$$V = 100*(2.53/7.6) \qquad \text{Eq. (6)}$$
$$V = 33.29 \text{ $/share}$$

McDonalds' actual closing price on January 3, 1997 was $45.00 per share. Does this mean that McDonalds' stock is overpriced at $45.00 per share? Not necessarily. The "Quick Value Estimate" is saying that McDonalds' stock is worth at least $33.29 per share based upon earnings alone. The critical factors of profitability, earnings growth, and inflation still need to be considered. Let's do this now.

The key measure of operating performance is return on capital employed. We measure profitability by using Return on Total Capital, (ROTC). (Total Capital is defined as equity plus long term debt). If a company's ROTC is higher than the AAA Corporate Bond Rate, its stock's Value should go up, and vice-versa. So let's include profitability into our equation for Value.

We have found that the effect of profitability is non-linear, and reflects reality as shown in the following equations:

$$V = 100*(E/I)*SQR(R/I) \qquad \text{Eq. (7)}$$

Where: SQR = Square Root
             R = Profitability Factor

16

$$R = I*SQR(ROTC/I) \qquad \text{Eq. (8)}$$

For McDonalds, ROTC - 13.3 percent. Therefore, starting with Eq. (8):

$$R = 7.6*SQR(13.3/7.6) \qquad \text{Eq. (8)}$$
$$R = 7.6*SQR(1.75)$$
$$R = 10.1$$

Substituting all the number into Eq. (7) gives:

$$V = 100*(2.53/7.6)*SQR(10.1/7.6) \qquad \text{Eq. (7)}$$
$$V = 100*(0.3329)*SQR(1.32)$$
$$V = 33.29*1.15$$
$$V = \$38.38$$

This looks a little better, but let's proceed.

Earnings growth is the key factor in perceiving future expectations. We need to compare earnings growth to inflation in the same way we compared profitability to interest rates. If a company's earnings growth rate does not exceed the current rate of inflation, it's falling behind and its stock Value should go down. We will also link earnings growth to profitability since profitability determines sustainable growth. Here is how it's done:

$$V = 100*(E/I)*SQR[(R+G)/(I+F)] \qquad \text{Eq. (9)}$$

Where: $G =$ Annual earnings growth rate in %/yr.
         $F =$ CPI inflation rate in %/yr.

Note that the factor, $SQR[(R+G)/(I+F)]$, is a performance measure of the company's ability to increase shareholder value. If this factor is less than 1.00, the company is losing out to interest and inflation and should be viewed as a questionable investment prospect.

For McDonalds: $G = 16.0$%/yr., $F = 3.0$%/yr, and

$$V = 100*(2.53/7.6)*SQR[(10.1+16.0)/(7.6+3.0)]$$
$$V = 100*(0.3329)*SQR(26.1/10.6)$$
$$V = 100*(0.3329)*SQR(2.46)$$
$$V = 100*(0.3329)*1.57$$
$$V = \$52.21$$

17

Inclusion of profitability and earnings growth in the valuation equation raised the calculated value of McDonalds from $33.29 per share to $52.21. McDonalds' closing price of $45.00 was between these two values. Which is the right answer? We should opt for the latter value. It's the result of a more complete assessment.

Now let's see how Equation (9) works for all the stocks in the DJIA. In Table I, we have listed all the data needed to use Equation (9), and have also converted the sum of the Values into the VV-DJIA using a divisor of 0.32481605.

Table I. Realistic Value Estimate of the Dow Jones
Industrial Stocks as of January 3, 1997. (I = 7.6%, F = 3.0%)

Stock	Price	EPS	ROTC	EGR	Value
ALCOA	68.0	4.29	14.7	-5.0	56.3
Allied Signal	69.0	3.91	19.9	14.0	81.0
Amer. Express	54.5	3.87	14.4	9.0	69.0
AT&T Corp.	41.5	3.46	7.6	9.0	56.9
Bethlehem Stl.	9.3	0.46	11.7	-6.0	5.4
Boeing Co.	106.4	4.48	3.9	8.0	66.4
Caterpillar	74.8	7.05	17.9	14.0	144.03
Chevron Corp.	66.1	4.23	11.7	17.0	87.9
Coca-Cola	53.1	1.60	46.5	17.0	38.9
Disney (Walt)	69.3	2.75	15.3	11.0	51.9
DuPont	98.1	7.05	25.8	13.0	148.0
Eastman Kodak	79.3	4.85	22.1	8.0	72.3
Exxon Corp.	98.6	5.37	13.8	3.0	79.0
Gen'l Electric	99.1	4.83	21.6	15.0	102.9
Gen' Motors	57.9	7.80	13.9	16.0	161.6
Goodyear Tire	52.4	4.83	14.6	10.0	88.0
Int'l BusMach	159.1	12.28	20.1	7.0	218.6
Int'l Paper	41.0	2.02	9.6	-8.0	21.4
McDonalds	45.0	2.53	13.3	16.0	52.2
Merck	82.6	3.49	25.6	17.0	78.5
Minnesota Mng.	84.8	4.12	17.2	15.0	85.6
Morgan (J.P.)	99.1	7.65	7.9	5.0	110.4
Philip Morris	113.0	8.62	22.9	17.0	191.4
Proctor & Gam	108.4	4.99	19.7	17.0	109.0
Sears	45.5	3.38	9.9	-2.0	40.2
Texaco	100.6	6.25	7.6	15.0	120.1
Union Carbide	41.6	4.80	27.3	-6.0	73.6
United Tech.	67.3	3.83	13.5	9.0	67.7
Westinghouse	19.4	0.39	0.7	5.0	4.3
Woolworth F W	21.5	1.50	2.8	4.0	17.8

DJIA . . . . . . 6544.0   VV-DJIA 7698.5

Does the VV-DJIA of 7,698.5 frighten you? It shouldn't. Taken as a whole, the companies in the Dow Jones Industrials have never been in better shape.

Eighteen of the DJIA stocks in Table I. have Value estimates above their January 3, 1997 closing prices and 12 are below. This shows that Equation (9) is not biased to give either high or low valuations. For the last several years, however, more stocks have tended to be undervalued as earnings have gone higher and higher.

In several cases the difference between the calculated Value and actual Price is quite large. This is an important signal that the stock is grossly overvalued or undervalued. For example, investors are expecting big things from Boeing since its Price is well above Value. On the other hand, Caterpillar, General Motors, IBM and Philip Morris are grossly undervalued. Overall, the VectorVest DJIA at 7,698.5 is saying that "irrational exuberance" has not unduly escalated asset values as Dr. Greenspan suggests.

It is also worth noting that as of January 3, 1997, the average Value of all 5,751 stocks in the VectorVest database was $21.89 per share compared to an average Price of $21.07 per share.

Our Purpose in valuing stocks is not to duplicate actual market prices with a formula. It is to determine what a stock's price ought to be based upon first principles. Equation (9) is a good start in this endeavor. Not only does Equation (9) give us the advantage of knowing whether a stock is over or undervalued, it does the following things:

- It allows us to relate the intrinsic value stocks to earnings, and to interest and inflation rates. It is the first and only stock valuation equation to bring these critical factors together in a realistic, usable fashion.
- It explains why highly profitable, high growth stocks command high P/E ratios, and
- It shows why P/E ratios must be assessed in light of prevailing economic conditions.

MAKE NO MISTAKE, THIS FORMULA ONLY GIVES "BALL-PARK" ESTIMATES OF A STOCK'S VALUE. Much better answers can be obtained directly from VectorVest. We analyze over 7,600 stocks each day for Value using a more sophisticated version of Equation (9). We've back tested our calculations to 1970, and tracked the Dow real time since 1978. We are especially proud of how well our model signaled the 1973-74 Bear market in November 1972, and the turnaround in late 1974.

19

Another exciting period was the valuation explosion exhibited by the VV-DJIA in late 1981...almost 12 months before the actual Dow took off in August 1982. This prescient behavior also was demonstrated in May 1987 when the VV-DJIA sank more then 350 points below the Dow signaling that, indeed, irrational exuberance was driving stock prices too high. Who can forget Black Monday, October 19, 1987 when the Dow fell more than 500 points?

The VV-DJIA signaled the 1990 Bear market five months in advance, but missed the big upturn of 1991. Indeed, long-term interest rates were still high and earnings were weak. When earnings did start improving, the VV-DJIA caught up to the Dow in late 1993, faltered in the 1994 down market and took off like a rocket in mid-1995. All in all, it's been an impressive journey, and it's not over yet.

Think of the tremendous advantage you have when you know how to value stocks.

Stock Valuation and
Stock Market Cycles

There is a terrific battle raging on Wall Street. The Bulls are looking for new highs. The Bears are saying the party's over. Both camps are making their point with a plethora of facts, fiction and fluff. How can we cut through this stuff and focus on what's really happening?

Astute investors know that three powerful forces drive the stock market. They are known to everyone, but often misunderstood. They are related, but independent. They are measurable, but controversial. They convey the effects of all that happens, and ultimately determine the fate of the market.

When a major event such as a product introduction, an earthquake, or assassination occurs, investors instinctively speculate on whether it will help or hurt corporate earnings. If the event seems likely to help earnings, prices rise. Conversely, prices fall if the news is perceived to be harmful. Corporate earnings is the first powerful force driving the stock market.

The bugaboo of a strong economy, and the thing that constantly haunts the market, is inflation. Inflation causes raw material, labor and service costs to rise.

21

Unless a company increases productivity and raises prices, profit margins narrow and earnings go down. Rising inflation ultimately pushes stock prices down. Inflation is the second powerful force driving the stock market.

Inflation not only lessens the value of financial assets, it erodes the purchasing power of consumers. Left unchecked, inflation destroys monetary stability, and leads to a weak economy. The Federal Reserve Board (The Fed) is charged with the responsibility of fighting inflation. It fulfills this task by controlling the money supply. When the Fed sees inflation increasing, it tightens the money supply, and interest rates go up.

Ironically, higher interest rates raise costs. It stifles investment, weakens the economy, hurts corporate earnings, and eventually leads to a Bear market. The third and most powerful force driving the stock market is interest rates.

In summary:

Stock prices rise when earnings go up. Stock prices fall when inflation rises, and stock prices fall when interest rates increase.

While most investors are familiar with these basic observations, the stock valuation formula published in Chapter 3 is the only relationship which ties them together. This relationship is shown as follows:

$$V = 100*(E/I)*SQR[(R+G)/(I+F)] \quad \text{Eq. (1)}$$

Where:
V = Stock Value in \$/Share
E = Earnings Per Share in \$/Share
I = AAA Corp. Bond Rate in Percent
SQR = Square Root
$ROTC$ = Return on Total Capital in Percent
R = $I*SQR(ROTC/I)$
G = Annual earnings growth rate in %/yr.
F = CPI inflation rate in %/yr.

Equation (1) clearly shows that Stock Value increases when Earnings Per Share, Profitability, and Earnings Growth Rate go up. Stock Value decreases when Interest rate and CPI inflation go up. Let's see how Eq. (1) can help us understand why and how the market cycles.

First, let's calculate the Value of the S&P 500 stock index to see where it stands today. As of September 23, 1994, the following data was available on the S&P 500:

22

$$E = 31.50 \quad \text{\$/Share}$$
$$I = 8.4 \quad \text{Percent}$$
$$ROTC = 10.0 \quad \text{Percent}$$
$$R = 9.2$$
$$G = 8.0 \quad \text{Percent/yr.}$$
$$F = 2.9 \quad \text{Percent/yr.}$$

Substituting these figures into Eq. (1) gives:

$$V = 100*(31.50/8.4)*SQR[9.2+8.0)/(8.4+2.9)]$$
$$= 100*(3.75)*SQR(17.2/11.3)$$
$$= 100*(3.75)*(1.23)$$
$$= 461.25$$

The S&P 500 closed at 459.68 on September 23, 1994.

Eq. (1) indicates that the S&P 500 was fairly valued. The race between higher earnings and higher interest and inflation rates was even. Neither Bull nor Bear currently had the upper hand.

Bull markets are born when the economy is very weak. Consider the most recent cycle. The Bull market began in October 1990 when the economic outlook was dismal and earnings were falling. That may sound absurd, but one must remember that interest and inflation rates were also falling.

The power of lower interest rates can be illustrated by noting that the S&P 500 index would rise 79 points (about 17 percent) if the AAA Corporate Bond rate fell only 1.00 percentage point. Obviously, when both interest and inflation rates were going down the market had extraordinary lifting power. This is exactly what happened in late 1990 and throughout 1991. It was the interest sensitive phase of the Bull market. Stocks of financial companies soared.

The economy began improving in March 1991, and earnings began to rise. Inflation and interest rates continued to fall, and the Bull market was in full swing. Stocks in housing, furniture, appliance, and other associated industries were on fire. It was the best of all worlds.

The Fed's last major move to lower interest rates was made in December 1991. The economy and the Bull market rolled on. Cyclical stocks such as autos and producers of large capital equipment were in vogue.

But things began to change with the subtle rise in interest rates in September 1993. The investment climate turned cloudy when The Fed tightened monetary policy in February 1994. We are now in a classic final phase of this Bull market. Stocks of commodities such as steels, paper and basic chemicals are on the rise. They are the last groups to see the boom in earnings. But the deadly duo of rising inflation and interest rates are also taking their toll.

Investors are torn between betting on the Bulls or going with the Bears. The game isn't over yet, but the economy will eventually defeat itself. The better the economy gets, the more it will force the Fed to raise interest rates. The Bull market will continue until stocks become grossly overvalued, and high interest rates strangle economic growth. Then the Bear market will come, and the cycle will begin anew.

Earnings Growth: The Golden Touch

Your job as an investor is to preserve and increase your net worth. Your enemies are spending, taxes, and inflation. Spending can be controlled. Taxes may be deferred, sheltered and avoided, but not evaded. Inflation cannot be deferred or evaded, but it can be overcome. One of the surest ways of defeating these enemies is to have a portfolio of solid growth stocks.

SETTING INVESTMENT OBJECTIVES. The rate of return needed to cope with taxes, overcome inflation and provide current income varies with economic conditions and your personal circumstances. Only you can decide how much cash you need for spending. Beyond the need for current income, the minimum rate of return you should aim to achieve is equal to the sum of the CPI inflation rate plus the yield on long-term AAA Corporate Bonds. In the early 1980's, this sum was about 20 percent per year. With inflation currently at three percent and AAA Corporate Bonds yielding about seven percent, it is now about 10 percent per year.

Stocks have appreciated historically at an average rate of nine percent per year. The average earnings growth rate for American companies also has been about nine percent per year. This is not a coincidence. Earnings growth is the engine that drives stock prices higher and higher.

The earnings growth rate of your stocks must be consistent with your investment objectives. If you want to double your money every five years, you should have a portfolio of solid stocks growing at least 14 percent per year. When inflation and interest rates increase, it's necessary to adjust your investment objectives accordingly. A thorough understanding of the role of earnings growth, how growth rates are estimated, and the appropriate use of growth estimates will help you select the right stocks.

THE ROLE OF EARNINGS GROWTH. Companies must grow to stay alive. They cannot stand still. Spending, taxes, and inflation erode a company's wealth just as they do yours. If a company fails to grow fast enough to stay ahead of these common enemies, it will eventually die. On the other hand, a company will prosper if its earnings grow steadily at a robust rate. Earnings growth is a manifestation of a company's health and future prospects. It is also a key indicator of your portfolio's health and potential.

ESTIMATING GROWTH RATES. The concept of earnings growth is very simple, yet estimating growth rates can be terribly difficult. It's like computing the gas mileage of your car. Calculating the MPG on a single tank of gas is very simple. But it can also be very misleading. Obviously, your average miles per gallon varies widely depending upon driving conditions and other circumstances. Companies like McDonalds and Coca-Cola grow earnings at a nice steady pace so there's very little problem estimating their growth rates. Other companies are like stop and go drivers. Their earnings go up and down in a hopelessly random fashion. Although it's virtually impossible to predict the earnings of these erratic performers, you still need to have an idea of their earnings growth prospects.

Given the variety of factors and circumstances affecting earnings performance, a system of estimating earnings growth is required that virtually tailors growth estimates for each company. Take, for example, the simple step of selecting a time period for computing a growth rate. When should the period begin? Five, ten, fifteen years ago? When should it end? One, three or ten years from now? This single decision makes a major difference in the growth rate estimate you would obtain. Other critical issues like handling negative numbers, and dividing by zero make it easy to see why many growth rate estimates may be totally erroneous.

One of the worst examples of misleading growth rates appears in a popular financial magazine which publishes monthly lists of "America's Fastest Growing Companies." These companies are defined as "showing at least a 200% gain in quarterly earnings." Sure, a company's quarterly earnings may increase from one cent to three cents for a 200% gain, but does that mean it's one of America's Fastest Growing Companies? Give me a break!

Statistical analysis of historical data is required to properly determine earnings growth performance. Earnings performance data may be obtained from a company's annual reports, or various financial services. Historical data is necessary but not sufficient. It only reflects the past. The stock market anticipates the future. Extrapolating the past to estimate future growth is a common and foolish mistake. You need forecasted growth rates to know where a company is heading.

VectorVest provides estimated growth rates for over 7,600 stocks every day. It statistically analyzes historical sales and earnings performance, takes into account current quarter-to-quarter changes in sales and earnings, and uses forecasted earnings to target future growth. VectorVest analyzes both sales and earnings to target future growth. VectorVest analyzes both sales and earnings data because they are linked in the long-term. Sales growth without accompanying increases in earnings growth reflects a loss of margin...a bad sign. Earnings growth without equivalent sales growth reflects cost cutting, productivity improvements and so on. These are good signs, but they can't last forever. Clearly, there's much more to estimating earnings growth than meets the eye.

USING GROWTH FORECASTS. Even a perfect growth estimate reflects conditions at a single moment in time. Therefore, it's necessary to use these estimates with three considerations in mind. These are:

1. Sustainability,
2. Trend, and
3. Variability.

SUSTAINABILITY. The mark of a great growth company is the ability to continue growing at a steady, predictable pace. The law of large numbers, however, dictates that extremely high earnings growth rates cannot be sustained. As a young company, Cisco Systems had an unbelievable run of triple digit quarterly gains. It was and still is a great growth company. But triple digit growth rates are no longer happening. The fruits of its own success made it so.

About one-third of the companies in our VectorVest database are currently estimated to grow at or above 14 percent per year. Many will still be growing rapidly ten years from now. Others will not. It takes phenomenal products, customer service and managements to grow at double digit rates for years on end. Coca-Cola, McDonalds, and Abbott Labs are prime examples of such great companies. They are literal money machines.

TRENDS. The transition from high growth to sustainable growth is a scary experience that usually causes considerable anxiety among investors. The slightest hint of an earnings slowdown causes a stock's price to fall. A failure to meet an earnings forecast by as little as one cent often results in a 30 percent drop in price. No one knows for sure what company's sustainable growth rate will be or when it will occur. Therefore, VectorVest updates its earnings estimates each week for every stock. VectorVest ProGraphics is the only software which allow you to see these trends on a chart.

We have found that long-term earnings growth trends provide excellent leading indicators of a stock's price performance. Wal-Mart Stores is a great company. It was a high growth stock, and its price went higher and higher. Wal-Mart's stock price peaked in March 1993 when its growth rate began to trend downward. It has begun to show renewed signs of growth recently, but no one knows whether its sustainable growth rate is 14.7 or 4 percent per year. Until this has been determined, Wal-Mart's stock price will lag the market.

Tracking growth trends may also reveal spectacular turn-around situations before they are generally recognized by the public. An unexpected increase in earnings performance often causes a stock's price to soar. This can happen even if a company loses less money than it did the year before. So a reduction in negative growth can be just as important as an increase in positive growth.

VARIABILITY. The third important consideration in using growth rates is that of variability. Premier growth companies have a history of consistent, predictable financial performance. It is very easy to estimate the growth rates of companies like McDonalds and Coca-Cola. These companies are called "Ruler Stocks" because their quarter-to-quarter earnings increase at a constant rate. You can lay a ruler along a plot of this data. Estimating that these companies will grow as they have in the past entails very little uncertainty.

The way to judge the variability, i.e., risk of a growth forecast is to examine VectorVest's Relative Safety ratings. Stocks with Relative Safety ratings above 1.00 on a scale of 0.00 to 2.00 have above average financial performance. They also have less variability in their growth forecasts. Less than 10 percent of the stocks in our database have growth rates greater than or equal to 14 percent per year, and Relative Safety ratings of 1.00 or over. Your chances of finding a "Ruler Stock" are even less. Let's see how this information can be used to build a variety of growth portfolios.

HIGH GROWTH STOCKS. Aggressive investors must deal with high growth stocks. The risks are high, but so are the potential rewards. Here's a list of the five fastest growing stocks currently in VectorVest's current database.

Table I. High Growth Stocks Ranked by Growth Rate in %/year.

Company	Price	Value	RS	GRT	$DIV	DY
Seachange Int	17.8	23.2	0.74	61	0.00	0.0
Yurie Systems	17.1	5.9	0.66	61	0.00	0.0
West CstEnt	4.9	11.3	0.71	57	0.00	0.0
Upton Resorc	9.5	16.5	0.89	53	0.00	0.0
Misonix Inc.	8.7	8.7	0.86	52	0.00	0.0

Data reflects 05/30/97 closing prices.

Value = $/share as computed by VectorVest
RS = Relative Safety
GRT = Earnings growth Rate in %/year
$DIV = Dividend in $/share
DY = Dividend Yield in Percent

Note the wide range of Price to Value comparisons among these stocks. This illustrates the uncertainty in assessing the potential of these companies. The low Relative Safety (RS) ratings also show the risks of dealing with unproven entities.

GROWTH & INCOME STOCKS. Conservative investors usually prefer to achieve their target level of total return by combining earnings growth with dividend payout. It's OK to do this, but don't take it too far. High yield without earnings growth is a losers game. I suggest that the earnings growth rate of your stocks be at least double the dividend yield. For example, a portfolio offering 12 percent total return would have stocks with at least eight percent growth and four percent yield. In most cases, I tend to favor stocks with higher growth and less yield. Here's a list of solid stocks with at least 11 percent growth and three percent yield.

Table II. Growth & Income Stocks Ranked by Growth Rate in %/year.

Company	Price	Value	RS	GRT	$DIV	DY
Alliance Cap	25.3	39.9	1.43	11	2.40	9.5
Hong Kong Tel	17.6	25.5	1.41	11	0.92	4.0
Ameritech	34.3	51.2	1.52	11	2.26	3.5
Natnwd HlthPr	17.6	25.5	1.18	14	1.56	7.3
BankOne Corp	16.1	19.6	1.18	11	1.52	3.5

Data reflects 05/30/97 closing prices.

Unlike the stocks in Table I., each of these stocks is undervalued, and has a solid track record of financial performance as reflected by the Relative Safety, (RS), values which are well above 1.00. Each company pays a dividend. The average sum of GRT and DY for these stocks is 17.5%. A lot of money managers would give their right arm to do as well.

RULER STOCKS. As noted above, the consistency and predictability of earnings performance of "Ruler Stocks" is so good that you can draw a straight line through their quarter-to-quarter twelve months earnings performance. They're easy to find with VectorVest ProGraphics. We simply ask the computer to find stocks having an RS>=1.40 and GRT>=14.

*Table III. "Ruler Stocks" Ranked by RS*GRT*

Company	Price	Value	RS	GRT	$DIV	DY
Microsoft	124.0	71.0	1.50	22	0.00	0.0
SunAmerica	47.3	67.6	1.45	19	0.40	0.8
Merck	89.9	82.9	1.58	16	1.68	1.9
Automatc Data	49.1	41.8	1.58	15	0.46	0.9
General Elec	60.5	51.3	1.40	14	1.04	1.7

Data reflects 05/30/97 closing prices.

Note that these phenomenal stocks are ranked by RS times GRT. (Only VectorVest ProGraphics can perform this search for you). Also note all of these stocks except SunAmerica are selling at a premium Price compared to Value. Why are they still worth buying? The answer will be given in Chapter 6, "High Growth vs. Low P/E Stocks." All of these stocks have favorable upside potential compared to an investment in AAA Corporate Bonds. Imagine seeing your money grow at an average rate of 17.2%/year with stocks in some of America's best managed companies!

PREMIER GROWTH STOCKS. Prudent investors want the best of all worlds...high growth and low risk. This marvelous combination can be found in premier growth stocks. These companies have exemplary records of above average, consistent, predictable earnings growth. Some pay dividends, some do not. Here's a short list of my favorites:

Table IV. Premier Growth Stocks Ranked by Growth Rate in %/year.

Company	Price	Value	RS	GRT	$DIV	DY
Cisco Systms	67.8	66.0	1.27	27	0.00	0.0
Nike, IncB	57.5	78.4	1.44	27	0.40	0.7
Sun MicroSys	32.0	53.8	1.28	26	0.00	0.0
Intel Corp.	151.1	253.4	1.40	25	0.20	0.1
Rotech Med.	16.9	27.0	1.43	22	0.00	0.0

With an average growth rate of 25.4 %/year, this portfolio of stocks has a good chance of doubling in three years. That's not a bad deal when you consider the relatively low risk of owning these stocks. Each is a leader in its field.

Coming up with these lists seems easy, but it's the result of a lot of hard work. Fortunately, VectorVest ProGraphics does all the work. All I had to do was decide what to ask VectorVest ProGraphics to do.

When it comes to preserving and increasing your wealth, go with consistent, predictable growth. It's the Golden Touch.

High Growth vs. Low P/E Stocks

High growth stocks offer the promise of the future. Low P/E stocks provide the certainty of today. There are strong arguments for and against buying either type of stock.

Which stocks are the best for you?

Many successful investors, including the legendary Peter Lynch, say a growth stock is fairly valued as long as its earnings growth rate is greater than its P/E ratio. David Dreman, the high priest of low P/E stocks, says that low P/E stocks provide better profits with less risk. These views are very interesting, but how can we tell which choice really is best?

Consider the following questions:

A. If someone were to offer you $500 now or $1,000 in three years, which would you take?
B. If someone offered to sell you a $1,000 not payable in three years, how much would you pay for it?

In regard to question (A), a lot of people would take the $500 now even though receiving an additional $500 in three years is very attractive. For whatever reason, $1,000 three years hence is deemed by these people to have a Present Value of only $500. Don't they know that $500 would have to grow at a compounded rate of 26 percent per year to become $1000 in three years? Maybe, but they want the money now. They are the kind of people that buy low P/E Stocks.

In regard to question (B), a lot of people would gladly pay $500 to receive $1,000 in three years. Compounding money at 26 percent per year is not chopped liver. That's what buying high growth stocks is all about.

Ah, but what about risk? Doesn't it play a role in making these decisions? Of course it does. It plays a very important role. That's why buying a stock simply because it has a high earnings growth rate or a low P/E ratio is not only naive, it's silly.

Unless one has a way of taking risk into account, they will never know how to make the best investment decisions. Discounted cash flow analysis provides the tools for doing this. It allows us to:

1. Calculate exactly how much money we should be willing to accept now (Present Value) in lieu of a future payment (Future Value) depending upon our desired rate of return and risk premium (Discount Rate),
2. Determine how much an investment should be worth in the future, and
3. Compute the Discount Rate for an investment given its Present and Future Values.

Let's apply these concepts to stock analysis.

When thinking about buying a stock, we're trying to judge how high its price will go knowing there is risk involved. In essence, we want to know if the price appreciation potential is worth the stock's current price and risk.

Here's how to get the answer:

I. COMPARE PRICE TO VALUE. In Chapter 3 we learned how to calculate the value of stocks. This calculation did not take risk into account or attempt to determine the future worth of a stock. However, it provides the necessary starting point for assessing a stock's price appreciation potential.

As we did in Chapter 3, let's consider our old friend McDonald's Corporation. Using the method described in Chapter 3, we calculate a value for

McDonald's of $54.20 per share. Its Price as of May 30, 1997 was $50.30 per share. McDonald's stock is undervalued by $3.90 per share which is good for the buyer. What we really want to know, however, is whether McDonald's will still look good after taking risk into account.

II. ASSIGN RISK. VectorVest performs a complete risk analysis on over 7,600 stocks each day based upon their financial condition, operating performance, stock price history and volatility. Because of its consistent, predictable performance, McDonald's has a very high safety rating in the VectorVest System of analysis. It has a Relative Safety of 1.57 on a scale of 0.00 to 2.00. It is, therefore, assigned a very low risk.

III. APPLY EARNINGS GROWTH TO PRICE APPRECIATION. We make the assumption that a stock's price appreciation will be consistent with its earnings growth over the long-term. Our work has shown that this is a valid assumption. For McDonald's, the forecasted earnings growth rate is 12%/yr.

IV. COMPUTE FUTURE VALUE. Given the Price to Value spread of $3.90 per share, earnings growth rate of 12%/yr, and Relative Safety of 1.57, we compute the Price of McDonalds three years into the future. It turns out to be $74.40 per share.

V. DISCOUNT FUTURE VALUE TO A NET PRESENT VALUE. This computation results in a number we call Relative Value. We use this term because Relative Value compares the price appreciation potential in McDonalds' stock, ($24.10 per share in three years), to the gain one would obtain from an alternative investment in AAA Corporate Bonds yielding 7.52% (The interest rate of 7.52% is our Discount Rate).

Since an investment in AAA Corporate Bonds would appreciate 24.3% in three years, the Relative Value of McDonalds' stock as of May 30, 1997 is: ($74.40/$50.30)/1.243=1.19.

A Relative Value of 1.19 says that an investment in McDonalds' stock would appreciate 19% more in three years than a comparable investment in AAA Corporate Bonds. Not bad for a stock with a growth rate of 12%/yr, and a P/E of 19!

Note that this very fine stock would fail both Mr. Lynch's test of Growth/(P/E) being greater than 1.00, (actually 0.63), and Mr. Dreman's test of having a low P/E ratio.

It is also worth noting by using Relative Value instead of Future Value, it is possible to compare all stocks on a consistent basis. Stocks with Relative Value

34

ratings above 1.00 have favorable price appreciation potential. Those with RV values below 1.00 are either overpriced, have low or non-existent earnings, and/or low growth rates.

If you want to have some fun and improve your profits, use VectorVest to examine the Relative Value and growth rates of the stocks you own. Discover whether you prefer high growth or low P/E.

Stock Safety: The Missing Link

I received a thing in the mail the other day called the "Hot Stocks Review." Phrases like "may even double again in the next twelve months," and "could have you crowing all the way to the bank" riveted my greedy eyes. Never one to pass up great investment opportunities, I decided to look into these "Hot Stocks." The blurb gave an 800 number to call for more information, but I prefer to do my own research.

The first thing I did was check my VectorVest database. Only two of the 29 stocks recommended by the "Hot Stocks Review" were covered by VectorVest. This was not too surprising since only eight of the 29 stocks are traded on American exchanges. Both of the stocks covered by VectorVest had a below average Safety rating. Neither had a Buy recommendation.

Neither of these stocks were covered by Value Line, so I checked Standard & Poor's Stock Guide which covers more than 7,600 stocks. Only one stock was found in this document. It was not ranked in terms of earnings and dividend quality.

Obviously, if one were to invest in any of these stocks they would have to believe the promotional material touting the stocks, or use the information sent by the companies. There are two problems here. First, it takes a lot of time and effort to analyze a company's financial statement, and I wasn't sure I wanted to do this even for the eight stocks traded on NASDAQ. Secondly, the investment caveats cited in company literature and prospectuses are designed to protect the seller not the buyer.

Of course, the publication featuring the "Hot Stocks Review" included the usual disclaimers that "all investments carry risks," and made it clear that "the publisher nor anyone else involved would be liable for any investment decision resulting from their recommendations." That's fine, but how does one get a handle on finding out how risky a stock is any way?

Risk has two Parts:
　　a. The probability of an unfavorable outcome, and
　　b. The consequences derived from that unfavorable outcome.

Simply put, investment risk entails the probability of losing money, and the pain associated with the loss.

Each of us needs to know how much money we can afford to lose on any single investment. We may be very comfortable, for example, with buying a lottery ticket even though the risk is extremely high because we can afford the loss. Buying stocks, however, is a lot different. We're using serious money when investing in the market...money that can make a difference in our lifestyles. Once we have established our "tolerance for risk", we can focus on assessing the risks involved with individual stocks.

Good information on stock safety is hard to find. Maybe that's because it's the last thing anybody want to think about. Even the few credible sources that provide some form of risk analysis, do so subjectively. Consequently, most investors do little more than plug intuition into their investment decisions. It's the missing link in assessing stocks.

Knowing how safe (or risky) a stock is can make the difference between making you a winner or loser as an investor. Here are the key factors used by VectorVest in assessing stock safety.

EARNINGS CONSISTENCY. The largest risk that shareholders have is that the company fails to meet earnings expectations. Experienced investors know that the moment of truth comes each quarter for every publicly traded American company. If a company fails to meet analyst's earnings estimates, its stock's price often drops 30% in a single day. Therefore, the single most important factor in assessing stock safety is in quantifying the probability that quarterly earnings will meet investor's expectations. If a company has a well established record of consistent, predictable earnings performance, it is much more likely to meet the market's expectations.

Companies like Abbott Labs, Coca-Cola, and McDonald's have exemplary records of consistent, predictable earnings performance. These stocks have very high Safety ratings in the VectorVest system of analysis. They also have favorable ratings in Value Line and in S&P's Stock Guide.

COMPANY SIZE. It is true that the stocks of large companies generally are safer than those of smaller companies. Many fund managers are forbidden to invest in companies with less than $500 million in annual sales. Obviously, larger sized companies aren't going to disappear overnight. Investors should not assume, however, that the shares of IBM, GM and Union Carbide are safe just because they belong to big companies. Size is not nearly as important to an equity investor as knowing where the company's earnings are heading. It is virtually impossible to forecast the earnings of IBM, General Motors and Union Carbide with any degree of accuracy. Therefore, the VectorVest ratings on these stocks are below average.

PRICE BEHAVIOR. The classic measure of price volatility is given by "Beta." Beta reflects the statistical movement of a stock price compared to the market. If a stock's price moves up and down exactly in sync with the market, it will have a Beta of 1.00. If a stock's price consistently moves up 10% more than the market and down 10% more than the market, it is more volatile than the market, and it has a Beta of 1.10.

Fair enough. High Beta stocks are more volatile than the market, and less predictable. Therefore, they are riskier than the market. Ironically, they are not necessarily riskier than some low Beta stocks. Certain stocks, such as gold stocks, are very volatile, but tend to move counter to the market. These stocks may have low or even negative Betas. Given this dilemma, I use Betas with a grain of salt. I prefer to analyze absolute price behavior to measure risk.

Absolute price behavior not only provides an unequivocal measure of volatility, but it allows one to assess risk in relation to the stock's price history. Since all things tend to move toward a mean, stocks which are above their price moving averages are more likely to move down, and stocks which are below their price moving averages are more likely to move up. Therefore, a stock which has moved well above its price moving average is riskier than one which has moved well below its price moving average.

LONGEVITY. It's better to deal with the devil you know, than with the one you don't. All other factors being equal, there's less risk in dealing with a company with a long track record than one which is brand new. Young companies offer some of the best investment opportunities, but they also bear potential pitfalls that could be fatal. Regardless of how good a stock looks, it's risky if it hasn't been traded for at least five years.

DIVIDEND HISTORY. A company doesn't have to pay a dividend to have a very safe stock. But if it does pay a dividend, it must maintain or increase the dividend without exception. A cut in dividend is a black eye for any company, and reflects poorly on its management and stock safety.

DEBT/EQUITY RATIO. The US government allow companies to deduct interest payments as a business expense. That's nice, but some companies overdo a good thing. They load up on debt beyond the point of being able to report any net earnings. Time Warner is a classic example of such a company. Its businesses are very good, but its balance sheet is a mess. Its Relative Safety rating in the VectorVest system is well below 1.00 on a scale of 0.00 to 2.00.

Beware of companies with excessive debt. Don't be fooled by the line about valuing a company based upon its cash flow. A company that can't report positive earnings after interest and tax payments is in big trouble no matter how you slice it. Safe stocks belong to companies with low debt/equity ratios.

OTHER FACTORS. The items cited above are only a short list of the many things that may be considered in assessing stock safety. Anyone who has studied accounting or read Benjamin Graham's book, "The Intelligent Investor," knows that there are many other things to look for. Regardless of how one might assess stock safety, it is important to do it systematically. Services such as VectorVest, Value Line, and Standard and Poor's use systematic approaches to assessing stock safety. Investors should always factor risk into their investment decisions.

USING STOCK SAFETY. Mr. Graham spends a lot of time in his book, "The Intelligent Investor," discussing the difference between investing and speculating. Basically, this difference is a matter of using knowledge to reduce risk to the point where the odds of winning are in your favor. Mr. Graham approaches the reduction of risk by advocating the purchase of undervalued stocks.

I approach valuation and safety as separate issues; then tie them together. In the previous chapter, High Growth vs. Low P/E stocks, I showed how valuation and stock safety are linked together in assessing a stock's long term investment potential. Both factors also play key roles in establishing Buy, Sell, Hold recommendations. Intelligent investment decisions cannot be made without including a knowledge of stock safety. Do not let stock safety be your missing link.

America's Safest
Growth & Income Stocks

Bull markets don't last forever. As the market changes with the economic cycle, investors constantly adjust their focus on how the primary forces of inflation, interest rates and earnings affect stock prices. When favorable inflation and interest rate trends turn sour, investors look to stocks with consistent earnings and dividends. Knowing which factors are driving the market is key to achieving outstanding long-term performance.

Ironically, the market performs best when the economic climate is at its worst. Consider, the Bull market cycle since 1991. Corporate earnings were terrible in 1991. But it was a great year for stocks. Why?

The weak economy in late 1990 and all of 1991 alleviated inflationary pressures, and allowed the Federal Reserve Board to lower interest rates. This caused money to flow from fixed income securities and saving accounts into stocks. Investors were anticipating, i.e., discounting, the arrival of better earnings. Stock prices soared. This was the "Discounting" phase of the Bull market. It lasted from October 1990 to February 1992.

Once the economy began to improve, investors became more selective.

They began turning away from consistent, predictable stocks such as foods and beverages to cyclical stocks that would see tremendous earnings gains. This marked a change in investor's stock choices, and is called the "Transition Phase." It lasted until February 1993.

The final phase of the Bull market was the "Capital Goods Phase" This occurred when the economy was gaining a full head of steam. The housing and automotive industries were running flat-out, and corporate earnings were soaring. It ended when everything looked great...on February 4, 1994.

The market topped on that day in February, and a new reality began to set in. As the Federal Reserve Board tightened money supply, investors could no longer count on lower interest rates to inflate stock prices. Just any old stock wasn't going to make it any more. As interest rates increased, it became increasingly difficult to find stocks that would hold up in the new environment. What kind of stocks performed best in the 1994 kind of environment?

Studies have shown that undervalued stocks with solid dividends hold up best in down markets. Over the long-term, dividends account for over 40 percent of the profits made in the stock market. Shrewd investors know that re-investing dividends is the surest way to accumulate wealth in the long-run.

The best of all worlds...collecting dividend checks while the prices of your stocks go up, comes from finding solid growth stocks that pay dividends. VectorVest is ideally suited to find these babies.

VectorVest analyzes and ranks over 7,600 stocks every day according to the following parameters:

PRICE	VALUE RV (Relative Value)	DY(%Dividend Yield)
RS (Relative Safety)	DS (Dividend Safety)	RT (Relative Timing)
DG (Dividend Growth)	GRT (Earnings Growth Rate)	YSG (YSG-Vector)
VST (VST-Vector)	EY (%Earnings Yield)	STOP (Stop-Price)
$DIV (Dividend/Share)	RISK (Low, Med., High)	REC (Buy, Hold, Sell)

The VectorVest Stock Advisory is especially useful to investors seeking growth and above average capital appreciation. Stocks with the highest VST-Vector ratings are deemed to have the best combinations of Value, Safety, and Timing.

The VectorVest Dividend Advisory is of primary interest to investors seeking current income and long-term profits. Stocks with the highest YSG-Vector ratings are deemed to have the best combinations of dividend Yield, Safety, and Growth.

VectorVest ProGraphics ties these products together via computer so that any of the above parameters can be used to screen, sort and rank stocks. We used it to find the safest, growth and income stocks in our database.

We asked ProGraphics to find stocks with the following characteristics:

Relative Safety >= 1.40
Dividend Yield >= 1.00
Earnings Growth >= 10
Dividend Growth >= 10

In the VectorVest system, stocks with Relative Safety ratings of at least 1.40 on a scale of 0.00 to 2.00 have outstanding financial performance. A Dividend Yield of at least 1.00 percent was selected to eliminate stocks with only token dividend payments. Earnings growth of at least 10 percent per year keeps us ahead of the sum of current inflation and interest rates, and finally, we wanted dividend growth to be at least equal to earnings growth.

We also asked ProGraphics to rank these stocks by the sum of VST-Vector and YSG-Vector. Stocks with the highest VST-Vector have the best combinations of Value, Safety and Timing. Stocks with the highest YST-Vector have the best combinations of dividend Yield, Safety and Growth. Stocks with the highest total VST-Vector and YSG-Vector should give us the best of both worlds. The top 10 stocks found by VectorVest ProGraphics as of May 23, 1997 are shown in Table I.

Table I. America's Safest Growth & Income Stocks
Ranked by VST-Vector + YSG-Vector

Company Name	Symbol	Price	Value	%DY	VST	YSG
AllianceCap	AC	25.60	40.30	9.40	1.32	1.43
United Asst	UAM	27.30	30.70	2.70	1.38	1.24
Old Kent Fnl	OKEN	53.50	72.20	2.50	1.37	1.24
Hong Kong Tel	HKT	21.00	28.20	3.70	1.35	1.26
Sherwin Wilm	SHW	29.50	33.10	1.40	1.36	1.25
Regions Fnl	RGBK	59.30	83.40	2.70	1.34	1.25
Kaydon Corp	KDN	49.30	70.70	1.10	1.36	1.21
Abbott Labs	ABT	64.00	60.60	1.70	1.35	1.21
Synovus Fnl	SNV	25.90	20.60	1.40	1.36	1.19
Wilmington Tr	WILM	44.60	62.40	3.20	1.30	1.25

Price = Closing Price as of 05/23/97.

Value = Inherent Value in $/Share.
%DY = Dividend Yield in percent.
VST = VST-Vector (Rating above 1.00 is good).
YSG = YSG-Vector (Rating above 1.00 is good).

Some highlights regarding the stocks in Table I. are as follows:

- The ten stocks listed above are currently undervalued. The Portfolio's average Price of $44.00 is well below its current Value of $50.22.
- Upside potential is excellent. The average Relative Value (not shown) of 1.35 is high on our scale of 0.00 to 2.00
- Dividend Yield is good. The average DY of 2.98 percent is well above the market's average yield of 1.47 percent.
- Earnings consistency and predictability is outstanding. The average Relative Safety (not shown) of 1.51 is very high on our scale of 0.00 to 2.00.
- Price performance is above average. The average Relative Timing (not shown) of 1.18 is well above the overall market which was at 1.02.
- Earnings growth is forecasted to be 13.2%/yr.
- Dividend Safety is excellent. The average DS value of 90 (not shown) ranks very high on our scale of 0-100.
- Dividend Growth is outstanding with an average DG (not shown) of 11.6%/yr.
- Dividend Risk is Low. The earnings pay-out is less than 50%.

In summary, this portfolio provides an enticing combination of low risk with above average dividend yield, dividend growth and earnings growth. In our book, it represents a fine list of America's Safest Growth and Income Stocks.

Timing: The Ultimate Weapon

"Desert Storm" was a piece of cake. By the time the Allied attack on Iraq was launched in February 1991, American reconnaissance had sliced and diced Iraq 80 ways to Sunday. Every significant target was identified and programmed into computers. The attack was spearheaded by "smart bombs." These guided missiles knew where to go and what to do. They epitomized the Allied force's supremacy in planning and running a high tech war.

The first truly successful smart bomb was an air-to-air missile called the "Sidewinder." It homed in on a heat source such as the exhaust of an airplane engine, and pursued it relentlessly. Very few targets escaped its destructive intent. For a while, it was the ultimate air combat weapon.

Just as military strategists search for weapons that can reliably seek and destroy enemy targets, investors look for sure proof methods of buying and selling stocks. Many investors apply the concepts of fundamental analysis. They analyze a company's business, its financial data, the economy, and other factors. They buy a stock when they are convinced they have found a bargain. These investors are called "Fundamentalists" or "Value" investors. They believe that undervalued stocks are recognized ultimately by higher prices, and are willing to wait a long time to be proven right.

Other investors are far less patient. They don't care a whit about a company's fundamentals or holding a stock for the long-term. They just want to buy low and sell high. They want to buy when a stock's price is about to go up, and sell when it's about to go down. How can they possibly expect to do this?

By reading the market. The market "tells a story," they say. The story is told by analyzing charts of price formations and patterns. The ability to read these formations and patterns allows one to tell whether prices will rise of fall, they claim. These individuals, called technicians, strive to predict future price behavior from historical relationships. If investors had a "guidance system" that would tell them when to buy or sell their stocks, they would, in fact, have the ultimate weapon.

A perfect timing system does not exist. But this is not to say that technical analysis is without merit. Quite to the contrary. Technical analysis plays a larger role in short-term stock market movements than fundamental analysis.

I have discussed the application of fundamental analysis to stock valuation and stock safety in prior chapters. So far, however, I have not mentioned technical analysis. While an understanding of stock value and safety are vital for appropriate stock selection, a knowledge of technical analysis and timing is essential for knowing when to buy and sell.

Designing a stock timing system is quite the same as designing a smart bomb. You need an analytical device that recognized its target, and a decisional mechanism to trigger an output. A stock timing system's analytical device, such as a chart, must recognize certain pricing patterns, and its decisional mechanism must produce an output signal to indicate whether the stock's price is rising or falling.

Exactly how one interprets historical price data, and produces an indicator depends upon their buy/sell philosophy. My philosophy is to buy a stock when it is going up in price, and sell when it is going down.

This philosophy may sound strange to many people, but it is grounded on the principle that stocks going up in price tend to continue going up, and stocks going down in price tend to continue going down. This philosophy is also consistent with the buying patterns of most investors. Investors flock to the market when it is going up, and shy away when is is going down. Favoring stocks which are rising in price is at the root of Value Line's celebrated timing system. It is also inherent in the "Relative Strength" approach to timing.

Relative Strength is simply a measure of a stock's price performance compared to the market. High Relative Strength stocks are those which are outperforming the market. Many extremely successful investors use Relative Strength as their primary timing system.

The trick with all timing systems is in knowing when a stock's price is going up or down. One of the simplest ways to analyze a stock's price behavior is to compare its price pattern to a moving average of its price history. If a stock's price is above its moving average price, and is moving away from the moving average, the stock is in an uptrend. The reverse is also true. VectorVest ProGraphics provides charting and moving average capabilities on over 7,600 stocks.

Investors who use moving averages to time their buy and sell transactions, can do very well. However, they will never "get in at the bottom," or "get out at the top" because of the nature of moving averages. On the other hand, good chartists can capture 70 or 80 percent of a move, and can avoid disastrous losses. And that ain't bad.

VectorVest computes (13 week) moving average prices for over 7,600 stocks each day. It publishes a stop-price for each stock based upon its moving average. Thus, if one sees that a stock's price is above its stop-price, they may conclude that the stock's price is above its moving average. But they would not be able to tell whether the stock is in an up or down price trend. This is done with an indicator called "Relative Timing."

VectorVest's Relative Timing, (RT) indicator analyzes the direction, magnitude and dynamics of a stock's price movement. It is reported on a scale of 0.00 to 2.00. When RT is above 1.00, the stock's price is in an uptrend. When RT is below 1.00, the stock's price is in a down-trend.

RT has all the characteristics of a guided missile system. Consistent with modern technology, it is extraordinarily fast. Once it locks in on a stock, it tracks the stock relentlessly. It explodes upward off of bottoms, and dives off of tops. It can see things not visible to the naked eye, and automatically returns to 1.00 when a stock's price flattens outs.

Since RT works within a framework of 0.00 to 2.00, all stocks may be searched, sorted, screened and ranked on a consistent basis. Week-to-week comparisons of RT, easily done by PC users with VectorVest ProGraphics, discovers many great winners just as they are beginning big moves.

No level of fundamental analysis could find these stocks at the critical point of eruption. They need not necessarily be undervalued, or of low risk. Investors must employ technical analysis and timing to complete their stock selection arsenal. Timing, it's the ultimate weapon.

Stop-Prices: Are They For You?

A Stop Price is like a pane of glass. Once it gets hit, it's broken. The use of Stop-Prices is one of the most controversial and misunderstood methods of selling stocks. Stop-Prices are two-edged swords. They can cut losses and protect profits, or result in high turnover and lost opportunities. Are they for you?

Selling is a crucial part of successful investing. Yet, it is avoided like the plague. The reasons are clear. Buying a stock is fun, a positive event. It's the beginning of a hopeful relationship.

Selling is a negative experience, the end of the relationship. Hope of future profits is gone, and losses become reality. Tax consequences must be addressed, and the proceeds need to be re-deployed. Selling is not fun, but it must be done.

While there are no hard and fast rules for selling stocks, each investor eventually makes decisions to sell. The need for funds, tax considerations, and a myriad of other factors enter into these decision. Whatever the reasons, the primary purposes of selling are:

1. To control losses, and
2. To protect profits.

Stop-Prices are ideally suited to do both.

STOP-PRICES. The term "Stop-Price" comes from the practice of selling stocks falling to specified prices. For example, if one of your stocks were at $27 a share, and you were concerned that it was going down in price you could place a "stop-loss" order to sell the stock at a specified price, say $25. In this case the Stop-Price is 25. Your broker would enter a "stop-loss" order to sell the stock if it fell to 25.

A "stop-loss" order does not guarantee that your order will be executed at the Stop-Price. The price at which your stock is sold depends upon market conditions. In severe downturns, stocks may be sold well below Stop-Prices. It is also important to know that "stop-loss" orders can be executed on exchange-traded stocks, e.g., New York and American stock exchanges, but not on over-the-counter (OTC) stocks.

In the event you own OTC stocks, you must use "mental stops," and monitor the prices yourself. You may find a "friendly" broker who will track OTC stock prices for you, but it is rare that a broker will do it. This is one of several drawbacks in dealing with OTC stocks.

Many advisors suggest that Stop-Prices be set at 10% below purchase prices. I have found that the Stop-Price of a stock should be based upon its safety, fundamentals, and price trend. Safe stocks with solid fundamentals should have "looser" Stop-Prices than those with weak fundamentals. These considerations allow investors to stay with solid stocks longer, and get out of weak stocks faster.

One of the major arguments against using Stop-Prices is that they result in excessive trading, and expose one's positions to "whip-sawing." The likelihood of experiencing these events depends upon the type of stocks one owns. Safe, steady performers rarely hit their Stop-Prices, while risky, highly volatile stocks often break their Stops.

Table I., shows the relationship between portfolio turnover rate in percent and stock safety.

Table I. Portfolio Turnover Rate in Percent per Year as a Function of Relative Safety.

Percent Turnover	Relative Safety
10	1.50
25	1.25
50	1.00
100	0.75
200	0.50

In the VectorVest system of analysis, stocks with a Relative Safety rating of 1.00 or higher, are above average in safety. Prudent and Conservative investors dealing in safe stocks would experience low turnover, while Aggressive and Speculative investors would have much higher turnover rates.

VectorVest analyzes over 7,600 stocks each day for Value, Safety and Timing, and calculates a Stop-Price for each stock. These Stop-Prices are based upon 13 week moving averages of closing prices, and they are fine-tuned according to each stock's safety, fundamentals, and price trend.

A stock's price behavior, and future performance can become vividly clear by observing the difference between a stock's price and its Stop-Price. If a stock's price is above its Stop-Price, and the price difference is getting wider on a day-to-day, or week-to-week basis, the stock is behaving favorably and will likely continue to perform well. If the reverse is true, the stock is heading for trouble. This is when you need to be on guard.

VectorVest alerts its users to these conditions by adjusting its Buy, Sell, Hold recommendations in the following manner:

A stock gets a "B" or an "H" recommendation if its price is above its Stop-Price, and it gets an "S" recommendation if its price is below its Stop-Price.

The distinction between a "B" and "H" recommendation is made on the basis of safety, fundamentals and price trend. Strong stocks receive "B" recommendations much more readily than weak stocks.

With this background in mind, let's see how Stop-Prices can be used to control losses and protect profits.

USING STOP-PRICES TO CONTROL LOSSES. The cardinal rule of investing is to keep your losses small. This goal may be achieved by virtue of the stock market's tremendous liquidity. It allows investors to specify both a buying price and a selling price at the same time. The best time to make these decisions is before buying a stock.

Investors should be aware that the period of highest risk is at the time of purchasing a stock. Taking commissions into account, you're already starting with a loss. If the stock heads down in price, the loss increases. The name of the game, at this point, is to control further losses. Stops provide the discipline to do this.

Let's consider our old friend, McDonald's. Suppose we wanted to buy McDonalds, and it closed at 41 3/4. VectorVest gave it a "B" recommendation, and a Stop-Price of $37.10. If we were to buy this stock at 41 3/4, we could also place a "stop-loss" order to sell it at 37 1/8. This would limit our downside risk to 4 5/8 points, or 11.1% of our purchase price not counting commissions. There are very few investments in which both a buying price and a selling price may be specified in advance.

The Stop-Price should be raised if the price of the stock goes up. Once the Stop-Price is above the purchase price, your risk of a loss virtually has been eliminated. Isn't that nice?

USING STOP-PRICES TO PROTECT PROFITS. As the price of a stock rises or falls, VectorVest automatically raises or lowers its Stop-Price. This information may be used to protect profits in a variety of ways.

1. THE RATCHET SYSTEM. The most conservative and, perhaps, the most common use of Stop-Prices, is to raise the Stop-Price as the price of a stock goes up. If one never lowers the Stop-Price, it moves only in one direction like a Ratchet. This system ensures that most of the profits gained from a price rise will be captured. It is, however, susceptible to premature selling and "whip-sawing." Consequently, the "Ratchet System" of using Stop-Prices does not necessarily lead to the best overall profit performance. This is the price one pays for reducing risk.

2. THE FLOATING SYSTEM. A slightly less conservative method of using Stop-Prices is that of allowing the Stop-Price to float up and down as the price of the stock fluctuates. This is very easy to do with VectorVest since new Stop-Prices are calculated every day. While this approach allows a Stop-Price to drift downward, it reduces turnover, commission costs, and the probability of getting "whip-sawed." While it may or may not provide higher profit performance than the Ratchet System, I prefer this method of using Stop-Prices.

When using the Floating System of setting Stop-Prices, one should never let the Stop-Price go below their purchase price once it has gone above the purchase price. Why encounter a loss when you had a profit?

3. THE GUIDANCE SYSTEM. Many investors prefer to use Stop-Prices as a guide to selling rather than a trigger for selling. They feel that Stop-Prices are too mechanical.

This approach to using Stop-Prices is perfectly satisfactory for investors who follow their stocks closely. Investors who work full-time or are traveling, however, are vulnerable to bad news. In today's age of instantaneous communication and electronic trading, a stock may drop 30% in an afternoon. The guidance system of using Stops is the least conservative method of managing one's portfolio. For the right investors, it may be the most profitable.

USING MENTAL STOP-PRICES. Many investors use Stop-Prices, but do not use stop-loss orders. They want more control over deciding when a stock is sold. This practice, called using "mental stops," is not the same as using the Guidance System of setting Stop-prices. For example, one may use the Ratchet System of setting mental Stop-Prices, and decide to use closing prices to trigger sell orders. This approach provides close rein over their portfolios, yet reduces excessive trading due to intra-day volatility.

Other investors use mental Floating Stops on a week-to-week basis. They generally have a long-term view of the market, but are also concerned about controlling losses and protecting profits.

As mentioned earlier, it is not possible to place stop-loss orders on OTC stocks. Therefore, one has no choice but to use mental stops. This is quite unfortunate. OTC stocks tend to be risky, many are illiquid, and have excessively wide Bid and Ask price spreads.

Whether you are a Prudent investor seeking an extra margin of safety, or a Speculative investor looking for trading points, Stop-Prices can help control losses and protect profits. Are they for you?

Investment Styles & Strategies

Thirty five years ago my wife and I attended our very first investment seminar. The speaker was from a large brokerage firm, and his mission was simple: Inspire us to become stock investors.

He spoke glowingly of Xerox, IBM and Texas Instruments, the great success stories of the late fifties. But he advocated buying low price to earnings ratio stocks. "Look how much more you get for your money by buying Ford with a P/E of 6," he said, "than you would if you bought Avon Products with a P/E of 40." It made sense to us, so we bought Ford. Six months later, Ford was down and Avon Products was up.

I talked to my broker about this, and he said that I should forget about buying individual stocks. I was new to the market, and should go into mutual funds. He suggested Techno Fund, a brand new fund chartered in the State of Ohio. He said Techno Fund was ideal for me since I was an engineer and it was investing in emerging technology stocks. It made sense to me, so I bought Techno Fund.

Eighteen months later, Techno Fund was defunct. The stock was worthless! Meanwhile, my brother had tripled his money in Erie-Lackawana, a bankrupt railroad, and my neighbor was bragging about how he was sending his kids through college by trading 1,000 share lots of stocks for profits of two or three dollars a share.

Through all of this, my instincts said that even I could make money in stocks. All I had to do was define my goals and put together a plan of how to do it. I knew I could not afford to be a speculator, and I didn't have the time to be a trader. I needed to buy stocks that I could live with. It wasn't easy, but eventually, things came my way.

The moral of this story is that every investor needs to define a realistic set of goals, the amount of risk they can handle, and a feasible investment plan. In my case, I wanted to double my money every five years, I was willing to accept modest losses, and I was going to invest in quality growth stocks.

Every investor has an intuitive sense of their own risk/reward profile. They feel it in their bones, and it dictates their investment patterns. Speculators and traders thrive on volatility and savor the thrill of making a fast buck. Conservative investors cringe at the thought of a capital loss, and patiently reap small rewards. Without knowing it, each of us has an investment style which is distinctly our own. A key to becoming a successful investor is in recognizing your investment style, and in buying stocks which are consistent with that style.

The VectorVest system of stock analysis identifies four basic investment styles. These are arranged in the following Strategic Investment Matrix:

STRATEGIC INVESTMENT MATRIX

R E W A R D	High	Prudent	Aggressive
	Low	Conservative	Speculative
		Low	High

RISK

54

PRUDENT INVESTOR. Prudent investors want the best of all worlds: High reward and low risk. They are interested in outperforming the market over the long-term, and achieving annual returns greater than the sum of long-term interest rates and inflation. The best way to meet these stringent requirements is to buy undervalued stocks with consistent, predictable earnings. How can we find them?

In the VectorVest system, these stocks are characterized by high Relative Value (RV) and Relative Safety (RS). All stocks in the VectorVest system are rated on a scale of 0.00 to 2.00. Investors buying high RV, high RS stocks are virtually certain of making money and outperforming the market in the long-term. A sample of these stocks is shown in Table I.

Table I. Selected Stocks for Prudent Investors (Ranked by VST-Vector)

Company Name	Price	RV	RS	RT	VST	GRT	REC
Intel	163.3	1.59	1.38	1.38	1.44	+25	B
Compaq Cptr	105.1	1.39	1.33	1.51	1.42	+18	B
SunAmerica	48.0	1.51	1.45	1.28	1.41	+19	B
Hong Kong Tel	21.0	1.35	1.42	1.29	1.35	+11	B
Wendy's Int'l	24.0	1.38	1.41	1.15	1.31	+16	B

Price = Closing Price as of 05/23/97.

RV = Relative Value
RS = Relative Safety
RT = Relative Timing
VST = VST-Vector
GRT = Earnings Growth Rate in %/yr.
REC = Recommendation.

Each of the stocks in Table I have an RV and RS above 1.00. This means that each stock has favorable potential for price appreciation, and an above average history of consistent financial performance.

- Intel Corporation is a powerhouse. It has the best combination of Value, Safety and Timing as indicated by the highest VST-Vector of 1.44.
- Compaq Computer's price is in a strong uptrend as shown by the Relative Timing, RT, of 1.51.
- SunAmerica has an excellent record of consistent, predictable financial performance as shown by the Relative Safety, RS, of 1.45.
- Hong Kong Telephone has a solid combination of indicators, and may see a strong uptrend in earnings growth, GRT.

- Wendy's Int'l has established itself as a steady growth company with a never ending array of new products and promotions.

AGGRESSIVE INVESTOR. Aggressive investors want high performance, e.g., capital appreciation of greater than 20 percent per year, and are willing to take substantial risk to achieve it. They are looking for big gainers and stocks with high upside potential. They typically like high growth stocks that are skyrocketing in price. These stocks are characterized by high Relative Value (RV), low Relative Safety (RS), and high Relative Timing (RT). Aggressive Investors are often associated with the "momentum" style of investing. Due to the volatility of high RV, low RS stocks, Aggressive Investors may substantially outperform or underperform the market over the long-term.

A sample of these stocks is shown in Table II.

Table II. Selected Stocks for Aggressive Investors (Ranked by VST-Vector)

Company Name	Price	RV	RS	RT	VST	GRT	REC
A S M Litho	55.0	1.44	0.90	1.72	1.41	+33	B
Yuri Systems	17.1	1.24	0.66	1.90	1.41	+61	B
Falcon Dring	45.4	1.61	0.82	1.56	1.38	+42	B
AmriCredit	19.1	1.54	0.98	1.48	1.35	+30	B
Jabil Circuits	61.1	1.11	0.87	1.79	1.35	+25	B

Price = Closing Price as of 05/23/97.

Each of the stocks shown in Table II has a favorable price appreciation potential, but above average risk.

- A S M Litho has the best combination of Value, Safety and Timing with the highest VST-Vector rating.
- Yuri Systems has the highest forecasted growth rate, 61%/yr, and is in the strongest upward price trend with an RT of 1.90. However, it is also the riskiest stock with an RS of 0.66.
- Falcon Drilling has the most favorable price potential with an RV of 1.61.
- AmeriCredit has a Relative Safety, RS, of 0.98 and may soon move to the Prudent quadrant of our Strategic Investment Matrix.
- Jabil Circuits formerly had the highest RV, but quadrupled in price in less than a year. Now it has a modest RV.

CONSERVATIVE INVESTOR. Conservative investors buy stocks, but do not like to take much risk. They are primarily interested in capital preservation, and are delighted to settle for average market returns. They typically buy low growth, steady performers which pay solid dividends. These stocks are characterized by low Relative Value (RV), and high Relative Safety (RS). Conservative Investors are virtually certain to make money over the long-term, but seldom outperform the market. A sample of these stocks is shown in Table III.

Table III. Selected Stocks for Conservative Investors (Ranked by VST-Vector)

Company Name	Price	RV	RS	RT	VST	GRT	REC
AFLAC Inc.	50.0	0.95	1.43	1.32	1.27	+5	B
Colgate Palm	59.8	0.95	1.37	1.27	1.23	+7	B
Pitney Bowes	70.9	0.90	1.22	1.24	1.15	+2	B
Otter Tail Pwr	31.3	0.99	1.24	0.90	1.05	+1	H
Seagram Co.	40.0	0.71	1.09	1.14	1.02	+0	H

Price = Closing Price as of 05/23/97.

Each of the stocks shown in Table III. has above average consistency of financial performance, but is overvalued at its current prices. None of these stocks are likely to outperform AAA Corporate Bonds over the next three years. Their steady, but lackluster earnings growth rates do not provide the thrust needed to outperform the market.

SPECULATIVE INVESTOR. Speculative investors are looking for big gains without regard to risk. The fundamentals of value and safety mean nothing to them. They buy stocks on hype and rumor, and are excited by price activity and volatility. Stocks with low Relative Value (RV), and low Relative Safety (RS) are unpredictable and volatile. Many of them are priced under $10. Nimble investors can make high profits in these stocks if they pay close attention to Relative Timing (RT), and to Stop-Prices. Without a keen sense of when to buy and sell, most speculators lose money over the long-term. A sample of these stocks is shown in Table IV.

Table IV. Selected Stocks for Speculative Investors *(Ranked by VST-Vector)*

Company Name	Price	RV	RS	RT	VST	GRT	REC
Manugistics	62.5	0.97	0.82	1.80	1.32	+29	B
Level OneComm	36.3	0.98	0.91	1.52	1.20	+18	B
Pure Software	15.7	0.77	0.72	1.37	1.03	+18	H
Warp 10 Tech	1.2	0.94	0.44	0.42	0.62	-7	S
EchoStar	12.6	0.17	0.46	0.21	0.31	-7	S

Price = Closing Price as of 05/23/97.

Each of the above stocks is highly priced compared to its inherent value, and has an erratic or unproven track record of financial performance.

- Manugistics and Level One Communications are rated "B" because of their high Relative Timing, RT, ratings. Moreover, they could move into the Aggressive quadrant with just a slight boost in Relative Value, RV.
- Pure Software is a pure speculation.
- Warp 10 tech and EchoStar are two stocks with big problems.

Prudent, Aggressive, Conservative, Speculative? Which of these investment styles rings your bell? Are your stocks consistent with your investment style and strategy?

Managing Your Portfolio

The players make the game. Everyone knows it...the owners, the players, and the fans. Baseball is a good example.

Regardless of how good managers are, they are not able to cause mediocre teams to perform like big leaguers. The best that managers can do is to help their teams fulfill their potential. Even with bonafide major leaguers, most managers fall far short of achieving this goal because of poor execution and bad decisions. In the end, the managers are no better than the players.

In the same light, many stock investors fail to achieve their goals for the same reasons. They buy losers, sell winners, make small profits, and suffer large losses. And they constantly underperform the market. How can we avoid these pitfalls, and make higher profits at lower risk?

STOCK SELECTION and TRADING TACTICS. Good portfolio management starts with selecting the right stocks. Just as major league scouts look for the best talent for their teams, investors should select the best stocks for their portfolios. This may sound like motherhood and apple pie, but the type of stocks you buy will dictate the manner in which you must manage your portfolio.

You cannot expect to outperform the market with conservative, overvalued stocks. Nor can you practice a "Buy and Hold" strategy with speculative, volatile stocks. The compatibility of your stocks with your management style is crucial to your long-term success. It is described best by using our Strategic Investment Matrix.

STRATEGIC INVESTMENT MATRIX

R **High**	**Prudent**	**Aggressive**
E		
W		
A		
R		
D **Low**	**Conservative**	**Speculative**
	Low	**High**

R I S K

This matrix was discussed at some length in the last chapter, "Investment Styles and Strategies."

The Reward/Risk coordinates of the matrix are defined quantitatively by VectorVest's Relative Value and Relative Safety indicators. Relative Value relates to Reward by indicating a stock's long-term price appreciation potential, and Relative Safety relates to Risk by reflecting the consistency and predictability of a company's financial performance. These indicators were also described in chapters 6 and 7.

For a variety of reasons, most investors prefer to "Buy and Hold" stocks for the long-term. Some of the advantages of holding stocks for the long-term include lower commission costs and fewer tax consequences. But it is not always the best thing to do. Even the best companies run into difficulties and their stocks should be sold. Other stocks in your portfolio probably should have never been purchased, and should be sold. How can we select stocks that can be held for the long-term?

Identify companies that do well in good times and bad. These companies have long records of consistent, predictable financial performance, low debt, high profitability, and solid earnings growth. Because of these characteristics, their stocks are very stable. These stocks all have high Relative Safety ratings in the VectorVest system of analysis. As shown in Table I., Relative Safety provides the key to how long one might expect to hold a stock.

Table I. Portfolio Turnover Rate in Percent per Year as a Function of Relative Safety.

Percent Turnover	Relative Safety
200	0.50
100	0.75
50	1.00
25	1.25
10	1.50

Investors dealing in speculative, highly volatile stocks with low Relative Safety ratings should expect to experience turnover rates well over 100 percent per year. Those investors buying low-risk, high Relative Safety stocks, will have very low turnover rates. Let's look further into the relationships of stock selection and trading tactics.

CONSERVATIVE STOCKS. Stocks falling into the Conservative quadrant of our Strategic Investment Matrix are ideally suited for "Buy and Hold" investors. These stocks belong to well established, dividend paying companies. They have below average Relative Value ratings, but are above average in Relative Safety.

Table II. Selected Stocks for Conservative Investors (*Ranked by Relative Safety*)

Company Name	Symbol	Price	RV	RS	DY	GRT
AFLAC Inc.	AFL	51.0	0.95	1.43	0.9	+5
Int'lFlavFrg	IFF	44.4	0.86	1.42	3.2	+0
Newell Co.	NWL	38.3	0.99	1.40	1.7	+7
Tyson Foods	TYSNA	20.5	0.77	1.40	0.5	+3
Bob Evans	BOBE	14.1	0.86	1.37	2.3	+0

Price = Closing Price as of 05/30/95.

RV = Relative Value on a scale of 0.00 to 2.00.
RS = Relative Safety on a scale of 0.00 to 2.00.
DY = Dividend Yield in Percent
GRT = Earnings Growth Rate in %/yr.

These steady, predictable stocks seldom receive a Sell recommendation. Investors buying Conservative stocks will experience low turnover, and low commission costs. Generally, however, they will also experience below average portfolio performance.

PRUDENT STOCKS. Prudent stocks offer above average capital appreciation potential along with above average safety. Investors buying Prudent stocks tend to hold them for the long-term, but also sell lackluster performers to improve profits. Therefore, their turnover is somewhat higher than a Conservative investor's, but their portfolio's performance is much better. Examples of Prudent stocks are shown in Table III.

Table III. Selected Stocks for Prudent Investors (Ranked by Relative Safety)

Company Name	Symbol	Price	RV	RS	DY	GRT
Hubbell Inc.	HUB/B	48.8	1.28	1.60	2.3	+14
Sherwin-Wllms	SHW	33.2	1.28	1.60	1.3	+14
Abbott Labs.	ABT	63.0	1.20	1.58	1.7	+14
Cracker Barrl	CBRL	29.0	1.41	1.57	0.1	+17
Fifth ThirdBn	FITB	77.3	1.27	1.57	1.5	+14

Price = Closing Price as of 05/30/95.

AGGRESSIVE STOCKS. Aggressive stocks have high upside price appreciation potential, but tend to be quite volatile. Investors dealing with these stocks must be willing to Sell when necessary to protect profits and/or minimize losses. The use of Stop-Sell prices is advocated strongly when managing stocks with Relative Safety ratings of less than 1.00. Portfolio turnover and commission costs can be substantial, but so can the profits. Some of our favorite Aggressive stocks are shown in Table IV.

Table IV. Selected Stocks for Aggressive Investors (Ranked by Relative Safety)

Company Name	Symbol	Price	RV	RS	DY	GRT
Pre-PaidLegal	PPD	20.1	1.43	1.00	0.0	+27
Dell Computer	DELL	112.5	1.43	0.94	0.0	+32
McAfee Assoc.	MCAF	65.9	1.31	0.93	0.0	+35
Delia's Inc.	DLIA	23.6	1.50	0.87	0.0	+51
Falcon Drlng	FLC	78.6	1.61	0.82	0.0	+42

Price = Closing Price as of 05/30/95.

SPECULATIVE STOCKS. These stocks are extremely volatile and demand close scrutiny and frequent trading. In my view, the use of Stop-Sell prices is mandatory when dealing with Speculative stocks. Turnover and commission costs will be high for traders, but the losses can also be high if one chooses not to sell when necessary. Table V shows examples of some very Speculative stocks:

Table V. Selected Stocks for Speculative Investors (*Ranked by Relative Safety*)

Company Name	Symbol	Price	RV	RS	DY	GRT
Howell Inds	HOW	34.9	0.76	0.97	2.9	-7
Boise Cascade	BCC	38.0	0.64	0.84	1.6	-6
Netcom On-Line	NETC	14.2	0.68	0.67	0.0	-11
Enamelon Inc.	ENML	17.6	0.06	0.57	0.0	-14
Omnipoint	OMPT	13.8	0.21	0.42	0.0	-9

Price = Closing Price as of 05/30/95.

DIVERSIFICATION and INVESTMENT TACTICS. It makes no sense for the average investor to try putting their eggs in a single basket, and watching them carefully. There are just too many uncontrolled variables in the stock market. Moreover, the average investor is the last to hear about bad news when it happens. I recommend that investors reduce risk by diversifying. This may be done by investing in a variety of different stocks in different industries, and by investing over a period of time. Don't plunge into the market all at one time. It pays to diversify.

The amount of money to put into any single stock depends, of course, upon your personal circumstances. As a rule of thumb, I like to see between ten and twenty stocks in a portfolio. Invest approximately equal dollar amounts into each of the stocks you buy. This is called "dollar weighting." It ties in with reducing risk by diversifying. While diversification is good, too much diversification will dilute your portfolio's performance and add to commission costs.

Don't be afraid to use margins. When used properly, margins can increase the profitability of your portfolio substantially. If one used prudent stock selection and effective trading tactics, the use of margins should not pose a problem.

THE BEST STRATEGY. When one takes into account the difficulty of picking winners, commission costs and tax consequences, the best strategy for the average investor is to create a diversified portfolio of high Relative Value, high Relative Safety stocks which require little or no trading. These stocks combine the best of all worlds, above average rewards and below average risks.

The Case For Using Earnings Yield

There is a very important number out there. But you won't find it in the Wall Street Journal, Barron's, or Investors Business Daily. Even Value Line, and Standard & Poor's don't provide this magic number. What is it, and what can it tell us?

The number is Earnings Yield, the kissing cousin of Dividend Yield. It's not used much in this country, so hardly anyone knows about it. But it's a dandy. It can be used to find forecasted earnings per share, assess dividend safety, calculate earnings growth rates, and determine inherent value. Let's learn more about it, and see how it can be applied.

EARNINGS YIELD VS. P/E RATIOS. A long time ago, a little gnome in a green eyeshade created Price to Earnings, (P/E) ratios. Gnomes love to think of everything in terms of ratios, and he was very proud of this one. This little gem, he thought, would tell investors exactly what they needed to know about the true cost of stocks. A $10 stock with a P/E of 18, for example, actually cost more than a $50 stock with a P/E ratio of 12. P/E ratios tell buyers how much they are paying for each dollar's worth of earnings. And that's what really counts...the bang for the buck. Obviously, the higher a stock's P/E ratio, the more expensive the stock. What could be better than that?

Consider Earnings Yield, for example. Earnings Yield tells you how much in earnings you're buying per dollar of investment, but it doesn't have any of the problems of P/E ratios. Yes, there are some problems with P/E ratios which we'll discuss. First, however, let's see what Earnings Yields are all about.

Earlier I said that Earnings Yield is the kissing cousin of Dividend Yield. Everyone knows what Dividend Yields are. They're published in all the papers, and investors use them to help make their investment decision. Just for the sake of clarity, however, let's note that Dividend Yield is defined as the annual dividend payment in dollars per share divided by stock price expressed in percent, i.e.,

$$DY = 100*(\$D)/P \qquad \text{Eq. (1)}$$

Where: DY = Dividend Yield in percent
         \$D = Annual dividend in \$/Share
         P = Price in \$/share

Our old friend, McDonald's Corp., closed on 05/30/95 at $50.30, and pays an annual dividend of $0.30 per share. Its Dividend Yield is:

$$DY = 100*(0.30)/50.3 = 0.60\%$$

The Earnings Yield for McDonald's based on trailing 12 month earnings of $2.30 per share is:

$$EY = 100*(\$E)/P \qquad \text{Eq. (2)}$$
$$EY = 100*(2.30)/50.3$$
$$EY = 4.57\%$$

Where: EY = Earnings Yield in percent
         \$E = Earnings in \$/Share
         P = Price in \$/Share

Obviously, there are no problems with calculating Dividend Yield and Earnings Yield for McDonald's. There is no problem in calculating its P/E ratio either. It's simply 50.3/2.30 = 21.9.

Is it any harder to think in terms of buying 4.57 cents of earnings for every dollar of McDonald's stock than it is to think of paying $21.90 per dollar of earnings? Maybe. But there are problems in getting P/E ratios for a lot of stocks. The first problem is that the P/E ratio of a stock with zero earnings is infinite. Now, that's not very useful. So the papers don't report it.

Why not report Earnings Yields instead? The Earnings Yield of a stock with zero earnings per year is 0.0%. This is very easy to understand. It clearly indicates that a company isn't making any money. Another problem with using P/E ratios is that stock with negative earnings would have a negative P/E ratio. I can live with that, but is seems the papers can't. So they don't report anything on stocks with negative earnings, either.

Does that mean, then, that every stock whose P/E ratio is not reported in the papers has zero or negative earnings? Definitely not. It seems that a stock has to trade for at least a year before the papers start showing its P/E ratio. This is unfortunate because new stocks often provide the best investment opportunities.

When everything is said and done, the P/E ratios of about thirty to forty percent of the stocks are not reported in the papers. This lack of completeness isn't necessary because the use of Earnings Yields would solve all the problems mentioned above. Table I shows examples of how Earnings Yield provides vital information when P/E fails.

Table I. Comparison of Dividend Yields, Earnings Yields and P/E Ratios of Selected Stocks. *(Ranked by Earnings Yield)*

Company Name	Price	$Div	DY	$EPS	EY	P/E
Cont'l Homes	16.4	0.20	1.2	4.64	28.3	3.5
Suburban Prpn	18.0	2.00	11.1	0.94	0.9	19.0
McDonald's	50.3	0.30	0.6	2.64	5.3	19.1
Laclede Steel	3.8	0.00	0.0	0.00	0.0	...
Cablevision A	32.6	0.00	0.0	-8.55	-26.2	...

Price = Closing Price as of 05/30/97.

$Div = Annual Dividend Payment in Dollars
DY = Dividend Yield in Percent
$EPS = 12 Month Leading Earnings Per Share
EY = Earnings Yield
P/E = Price to Earnings Ratio as Reported by VectorVest.

A final problem with relying on P/E ratios for information is that P/E ratios are typically based upon trailing twelve month earnings. While this is better than not having any information at all, the market is not driven by trailing earnings. It is driven by forecasted earnings. Wouldn't it be nice to know what the forecasted earnings are for the stocks you own?

EARNINGS YIELD AND EARNINGS FORECASTS. A number of services provide information on earnings forecasts. Getting this information can be expensive, however. Not getting it, could be even more expensive. So I buy the information, and use it in VectorVest to compute earnings growth rates, assess dividend safety and calculate stock value. However, I don't use raw earnings forecasts. I tailor them to meet my needs.

I create an estimate of leading 12 month earnings. Earnings estimates are usually rolled into a calendar year or fiscal year. These estimates are subject to change, and cause variation in our assessments. The use of 12 month leading earnings reduces this variation, and is more reliable than using raw forecasts.

Earnings Yields based on leading 12 month earnings estimates are published for over 7,600 stocks in VectorVest ProGraphics. All that one needs to do to get a 12 month leading earnings estimate from Earnings Yield as reported by VectorVest is use the following equation:

$$\$E = (P*EY)/100 \qquad\qquad \text{Eq. (3)}$$

Where: $\$E$ = 12 Month Leading Earnings
P = Price in \$/Share
EY = Earnings Yield in Percent

The Earnings Yield for McDonald's Corp. as reported by VectorVest is 5.25%. Therefore, it would have a 12 month leading earnings estimate of \$2.64 per share.

This valuable bit of information can be used in several ways. It can be used in assessing dividend safety, estimating growth rates and stock valuation. We'll illustrate how these things can be done in the next chapter when we complete **THE CASE FOR USING EARNINGS YIELDS.**

The Earnings Yield: The Magic Number

If there's one thing you should know about a stock, it is its Earnings Yield. This vital bit of information leads to several important and revealing insights. It's the magic number.

In the last chapter, we presented "The Case for Using Earnings Yield." We discussed the advantages of using Earnings Yield compared to P/E ratios, and showed how to get forecasted earnings from VectorVest's Earnings Yield data. This month, we will illustrate how Earnings Yield may be used to assess dividend safety, estimate earnings growth rates, and analyze stock value.

ASSESSING DIVIDEND SAFETY. You may recall that we referred to Earnings Yield as the kissing cousin of Dividend Yield. Since Earnings Yield reflects the amount of money a company is making, and Dividend Yield reflects the amount of money being paid out to shareholders, Earnings Yield provides an ideal tool for assessing dividend safety. It's simply a matter of comparing one to the other.

All investors should realize that a company's dividend payments are no safer than its earnings performance. Dividends cannot be paid out of thin air. Eventually, they must come from earnings. If the Dividend Yield exceeds the

Earnings Yield, there's trouble in River City. The best way, then, of judging the viability of a company's dividend payments is to measure the percentage of earnings being paid out as dividends.

The proportion of earnings paid out as dividends is called the Dividend Payout. This is determined as follows:

$$DP = (DY/EY)*100 \qquad \text{Eq. (1)}$$

Where: DP = Dividend Payout in Percent
          DY = Dividend Yield in Percent
          EY = Earnings Yield in Percent

A Dividend Payout of about 35% is considered to be normal, safe and reasonable. Anything about 50% is usually regarded as excessive, and less likely to be maintained. Let's use VectorVest ProGraphics to examine the Dividend and Earnings Yield relationships of some stocks and industry groups.

VectorVest ProGraphics allows us to sort, screen, search and rank over 7,600 stocks and 190 industry groups by Earnings Yield and Dividend Yield. It also provides a dividend risk assessment of Low, Medium or High for each stock. Here's a summary of a few interesting selections ranked in ascending order of Dividend Payout.

Table I. Selected Stocks Ranked by Dividend Payout.

Company Name	Price	$Div	DY	EY	DP	Risk
McDonald's	50.3	0.30	0.6	5.3	12.7	Low
Pitney Bowes	70.3	1.60	2.3	5.3	43.3	Med
Consol NatGas	53.1	1.94	3.7	6.5	56.9	Med
Southwest Gas	17.1	0.82	4.8	5.6	85.7	High
Hlth CarePpty	33.0	2.44	7.2	5.0	144.0	High

Price = Closing Price as of 05/30/97.

$Div = Annual Dividend Payment in Dollars
 DY   = Dividend Yield in Percent
 EY   = Earnings Yield in Percent based upon 12 Month Leading
         Earnings Estimate
 DP   = Dividend Payout in Percent
 Risk = Risk Assessment as determined by VectorVest

Obviously, there is a direct correlation between Dividend Payout and Dividend Risk. McDonald's is virtually certain to maintain or increase its dividends while Southwest Gas and Health Care Properties may very well do the opposite.

Of course, there's a lot more to assessing dividend safety than just comparing Earnings and Dividend Yields, but it's and awfully good place to start. Consider the Electric Power Industry, for example.

The 96 Electric Power utility companies which we track have an average Dividend Yield of 5.8%, and an average Earnings Yield of 8.9%. They are paying out 65.2% of earnings as dividends. Where are they going to get the money to keep paying these dividends, and still stay in business? Something's got to give, and it's probably the dividend payments.

ESTIMATING EARNINGS GROWTH RATES. A pretty good estimate of a company's earnings growth rate can be made by using Earnings Yields based upon 12 month leading earnings, and P/E ratios based upon trailing 12 month earnings. The computation is very simple:

$$EGR = 100*(LE-TE)/TE \qquad \text{Eq. (2)}$$

Where: EGR = Earnings Growth Rate in Percent
LE = 12 Month Leading Earnings
TE = 12 Month Trailing Earnings

Since   LE = (P*EY)/100   Eq. (3)
and   TE = P/(P/E)   Eq. (4)

$$EGR = 100*[(P*EY)/100-(P/(P/E))]/[(P/(P/E))] \qquad \text{Eq. (5)}$$

Where: P = Price in $ per Share
EY = Earnings Yield in Percent
P/E = Price to Earnings Ratio

Using the data shown for McDonald's in Table I, and a P/E ratio of 21.9 as cited in Chapter 13, the Earnings Growth Rate (EGR) for McDonald's is:

$$EGR = 100*[(50.3*5.3)/100-(50.3/21.9)]/(50.3/21.9)$$
$$= 100*[(2.66-2.30)]/2.30 = 15.7\%$$

Not bad! This estimate compares extremely well to our current 1 to 3 year estimate of 12 percent per year. Try it on a few stocks of your own. You'll be amazed how well it works.

ESTIMATING GROWTH TO P/E RATIOS. The biggest and best of professional money managers, including Peter Lynch, use Growth to P/E ratios (GPE) as a measure of valuation. When the GPE is above 1.00, a stock is deemed to be undervalued. When GPE is less than 1.00, it is deemed to be overvalued.

Consider the GPE ratio for McDonald's. It has an estimated Earnings Growth Rate of 12, and a leading P/E ratio of 19. Therefore:

$$GPE = 12/19 = 0.63$$

The GPE ratio of 0.63 says that McDonald's stock is overvalued by 37 percent. It very well might be. McDonald's has an exemplary track record, and should be selling at a premium. But our studies show the GPE's are not perfect measures of valuation. Actually our calculations of Relative Value (RV) are far more sophisticated measures of valuation. The RV for McDonald's was 1.19 as of May 30, 1997. (See Chapter 6 for more on this subject).

We're not done using Earnings Yield yet. Let's examine another simple, but better method of estimating inherent value.

ESTIMATING INHERENT VALUE. In Chapter 3 we illustrated the use of a "Quick Value Estimate" equation for calculating inherent value. It simply requires one to divide annual earnings per share by the AAA Corporate Bond rate. Thus:

$$V = 100*(E/I) \hspace{3cm} \text{Eq. (6)}$$

Where: V = Value of a Stock in $/share
                E = Earnings in $/share
                I = AAA Corporate Bond Rate in Percent

Since $E = (EY*P)/100$ Eq. (7)

then $V = 100*[(EY*P)100]/I$
           $= (EY*P)/I$ Eq. (8)

Using a AAA Corporate Bond Rate of 7.53%, and the data shown in Table I, the Value for McDonald's is:

$$V = (5.3*50.3)/7.53$$
$$= \$35.4 \text{ per share}$$

By golly, this is 70% of McDonald's May 26th closing Price compared to the 67% level obtained from the GPE analysis. Maybe McDonald's is overvalued after all!

Wow! Let's see where we're at. Earnings Yield gives us something that's:

1. More informative than P/E ratios,
2. Can give us 12 month leading earnings estimates,
3. Can be used to assess Dividend Safety,
4. Can be used to estimate Earnings Growth Rates,
5. Can be used to get Growth to P/E ratios, and
6. Can be used to get an estimate of Inherent Value.

All from one number. It's magic.

About ten years ago VectorVest created a *"Guide to Worry-Free Investing"* which embodies the principles discussed in this article. You may receive a FREE copy of this guide by calling 1-330-668-2814.

Bottom Fishing: The Art Of Buying Low and Selling High

With a new generation of gunslingers driving stock prices higher and higher, how can we find low-priced bargains? By bottom fishing, of course. It's the art of buying low and selling high, and a great way to get rich. Why isn't everybody doing it?

Buying low and selling high is not as easy as it sounds. No one knows for sure which stocks are "low," and which are "high." A stock that seems "low" may go lower. One that seems "high" may go higher. How can we tell which is likely to do what?

Clearly, history can be our guide. A stock whose price has fallen from a peak is "low" relative to that peak. A peak may reflect the highest price a stock has ever attained, or it may reflect an intermediate high over the last 52 or 13 weeks. Whatever the case may be, investors perceive that stocks are "low" when their prices are down from former levels, and "high" when prices have risen from lower levels.

Ideally, one would like to buy good stocks that have been beaten down in price and are poised to rise. Here's how to play the game.

I. IDENTIFY STOCKS THAT ARE "LOW" IN PRICE. This is very easy to do. Virtually every newspaper that publishes stock prices indicates those which have hit 52 week lows. The Wall Street Journal and Investors Business Daily print lists of these stocks each day. Barron's Magazine prints a comprehensive weekly list of stock's hitting 52 week lows.

Computer literate investors have access to a virtual storehouse of historical data from a wide variety of sources. Computers provide the most convenient and efficient way of finding stocks hitting new lows. They are also most useful in creating "watch lists" for further analysis and tracking. VectorVest ProGraphics, stock analysis software program creates "watch lists" of stocks hitting new lows for any period ranging from one week to 52 weeks.

II. SELECT STOCKS MOST LIKELY TO REBOUND. This task gets to the heart of one's bottom fishing skills. The key here is to use a few critical criteria to find good stocks that have been beaten-down to bargain prices. Another objective of this selection process is to winnow a large number of stocks to a manageable few which can be tracked on a watch list.

Computer screening allows investors to use a wide variety of criteria to find the most desirable stocks. If one does not have a computer, however, this winnowing process can be done manually.

Many investors suggest that investors favor stocks with the lowest Price to Earnings ratios. This is not a bad place to start, and is very easy to do. On a weekly basis you can select, say, the 10 stocks with the lowest P/E ratios which have hit 52 week lows, and put them on your watch list.

Another equally simple, but much more powerful screen can be conducted by using The VectorVest Stock Advisory to select stocks with the highest Value-Safety-Timing Vector. Some of the stocks we've discovered using this system include Dollar General, up 36% in seven weeks, Andrew Corp., up 40% in eight weeks, and Brandon Systems, up 49% in 18 weeks.

Once this initial screening process is completed, find out why the stock's price is going down. There's always a reason why a stock is moving down. Is the company suffering from weaker sales? Is it experiencing slimmer profit margins? Seeing slower earnings growth? If so, scratch it off your list. Is the company doing well but suffering "guilt by association" in an industry which is out of favor? Does it have good fundamentals? If so, you've got a potentially big winner. Stocks with good fundamentals go up sooner, faster and farther than stocks with weak fundamentals.

III. BUY STOCKS THAT ARE RISING IN PRICE. This may sound
like a contradiction, but it's the most important part of bottom fishing. Never
buy stocks on the way down! Nobody knows how low they can go or how long
they will stay down. Remember, the oil drilling stocks? They were the hottest
things around in the early 1980's...until they got killed. It has taken 15 years for
them to come back. That's a long time to wait.

One would love, of course, to buy stocks at the exact bottoms. But buying a
stock on the way down is like catching a falling sword. Micron Technology hit
a high of 94 3/4 in the summer of '95. Our VectorVest Stop-Price was 76 5/8.
When Micron crashed through the Stop, it got a Sell Recommendation. Some
people thought it was bargain at 70. Others thought it was a steal at 60. Still
others thought it had hit bottom at 40. It never stopped falling until it hit 18 1/2
in July 1996. Micron has finally bounced back and received a Buy
recommendation in September 1997 at 31 1/8. Sure, we may have missed the
bottom price of 18 1/2, but there were a lot of better fish in the ocean than
Micron Technology.

How can we tell when a stock has stopped falling in price? The best way is
to use computerized charting techniques. If a stock's price has fallen below its
13 week moving average, it is in a downtrend. If it has consolidated and risen
above its 13 week moving average, it has reversed the downtrend and may have
started a sustained uptrend. Aggressive investors may prefer to use short-term
moving averages, such as 50 day moving averages. Conservative investors
prefer to use 200 day moving averages. Some characters use a combination of
moving averages. VectorVest ProGraphics allows you to track price
performance using two simultaneous moving averages. I like to use a
combination of a 13 week and 26 week moving averages for long-term
investing, and a 5 day and 10 day combination for trading.

Investors who don't have computers may get an idea of a stock's price trend
by comparing a stock's current price to its 52 week range. For example, Micron
Technology closed on Friday May 30, 1997 at 42 1/4, up 128.4% from its 52
week low of 18 1/2 and only 6.6% below its 52 week high 45 1/4. By this
measure Micron Tech clearly bottomed at 18 1/2, but VectorVest still doesn't
like it. VectorVest knows that Micron's stock is overvalued and the risks of
owning MU are high.

VectorVest ProGraphics is ideally suited for bottom fishing. Every stock in
the VectorVest system receives an "S" Recommendation when its price falls
below its Stop-Price. Stocks with prices above their Stop-Prices receive "H" or
"B" Recommendations. All Stop-Prices are computed from 13 week price
moving averages. Stocks making a "turnaround" from an "S" to a "B" are, in all

likelihood, still near recent lows. Buying good stocks just as they start moving up is what "Bottom Fishing" is all about.

VectorVest ProGraphics, our computer software program, allows us to conduct a wide variety of bottom fishing strategies with remarkable ease and convenience. Consider the following strategy: We asked VectorVest ProGraphics to find, week-by-week, all the stocks hitting 26 week lows for the period 09/22/95 to 02/23/96. Each week we put the top 10 stocks ranked by Value-Safety-Timing Vector into a "WatchList." Whenever one of these stocks got a "B" Recommendation, we bought it. If it subsequently got an "S" Recommendation, we sold it. Here are the results:

- Over the five month period, 126 stocks were added to the "WatchList."
- Seventy four stocks subsequently received "B" Recommendations.
- Sixty three of these stocks are still active with an annualized gain of 39.9%.
- Eleven stocks were sold with an average loss of 9.6%.

On the same basis, the S&P 500 index gained 23.3%. As you can see, about six out of seven VectorVest recommendations were profitable.

We've done a number of bottom fishing studies using VectorVest ProGraphics with even better results. One of our favorite strategies involved picking the best stocks in industries coming off of bottoms. It produced a documented annualized gain of 68.9%!

We found that bottom fishing not only provides opportunities for outstanding profits, but it also reduces downside risk. It makes one believe that bargains still abound, and that bottom fishing, is indeed, the art of buying low and selling high.

Teeny Boppers: Low Price Stocks with Explosive Price Appreciation Potential

On January 20, 1995 I published a list of 50 Buy rated stocks called "High Performers." This list included Micron Technology which went from 22 5/8 to 94 3/4, US Robotics, from 23 1/2 to 179, and Ascend Communications, from 6 to 62. My favorite, however, is Iomega which went from a split adjusted 1 11/16 to 66, up a fantastic 3,800 percent! How did I find these stocks?

Very simple. I was tracking stocks that were hitting new 52 week highs, and ranking them according to a certain system I have. Before getting into that, however, let's step back a minute.

Why was I tracking stocks that were hitting 52 week highs? In the last chapter on "Bottom Fishing," I extolled the virtues of buying low and selling high, and suggested the idea of tracking stocks hitting 52 week lows. Now I'm saying the opposite. Have I lost my marbles?

Not really. The approach we described works very well, but it's not only way to make money in the stock market. In fact, the method of finding low-priced stocks having explosive price appreciation potential described in this article has a lot in common with the last chapter.

In both cases we're tracking stocks which are deviating significantly from their normal patterns, i.e., they're making 52 week lows or 52 week highs. These stocks are screaming for attention. They're telling us that something significant, good or bad, is happening. We ought to be able to take advantage of these situations.

Another common point, and a very important one I might add, is that I advocate buying stocks that are rising in price whether you are bottom fishing or not. A critical key to successful Bottom Fishing is buying these stocks AFTER they have stopped going down. I never buy a stock on the way down. If you're good, you can catch depressed stocks just as they have started going up...usually within 10-15 percent of their lows.

An easier game to play, however, is buying stocks that are hitting new highs. Think of this: Iomega didn't go from 1 11/16 to 66 without hitting new highs time after time. It was screaming for attention. All we had to do was listen to it.

Many studies show that one of the surest ways of making money in the stock market is to buy stocks hitting new highs. A lot of people, however, don't like to do this because they think these stocks are "over-bought" or "over-extended." Nonsense. I've seen too many stocks take-off and never return to their so called buying ranges. Many people resist buying stocks hitting new highs because the big guys, i.e., high-priced stocks, get all the attention. This problem is easily solved by buying low-priced stocks hitting new highs. I call these stocks "Teeny Boppers."

Teeny Boppers remind me of teenagers. They are full of energy, vigor and ambition. They have new ideas, and different ways of doing things. They represent the wave of the future, but are untested. They're risky, and many fail to fulfill their promise. But many succeed. When they do, they become our new leaders. Iomega was a classic Teeny Bopper. Here's how to find the next Iomega.

I. IDENTIFY LOW-PRICED STOCKS HITTING NEW HIGHS. There are no hard and fast rules for defining low-priced stocks, but let's restrict our discussion to stocks under $6.00. These stocks can be found with a computer or in various financial publications. If you don't have a computer, I suggest using Barron's magazine. It publishes a weekly summary of the market, and identifies stocks hitting new highs by putting an "up" arrow before the 52 week price range. Unfortunately, this indicator is not used in Barron's list of NASDAQ Small-Cap Stocks. (We'll handle this problem later).

All you need to do is go down the lists of stocks in the various exchanges on a week-by-week basis, and mark every stock under $6.00 which has hit a 52 week high. *SAVE THIS WORK!* We'll need to winnow these stocks to a manageable few.

II. DEVELOP A SHORT LIST OF SELECTIONS. Stocks with explosive price potential have staying power. By this, I mean they will make new highs again and again and again. As you go through your weekly routine of marking the stocks making new highs, you'll notice that from week-to-week many of these stocks will appear a second, third or more times. Note that it is not necessary for a stock to hit new highs in consecutive weeks. Once a stock has made a new high for the third time, however, give it special attention. Mark it in a special way. If it appears a fourth time, write it down on a 3 x 5 card, and begin to analyze it.

III. ANALYZE YOUR SELECTIONS AND MAKE YOUR FINAL CHOICES. Put a summary of each stock's weekly price history on your 3 x 5 cards, and include other information such as its P/E ratio, weekly trading volume, and quarterly earnings performance. You can get all this information from Barron's. Of course, you are free to consult any other information sources at your disposal. Investors Alliance's Power Investor for Windows and its DOS based Stock Market Database provide comprehensive sources of information at very low cost.

In any event, you must recognize that analyzing low-priced stocks on the basis of fundamentals often becomes an exercise of faith. Most low-priced stocks have very weak fundamentals. So it's worth learning as much as you can about the company's products, services, and potential. Call the company to find out what makes it attractive to investors other than current earnings per share. Visit VectorVest's web site at: **www.vectorvest.com** for a **FREE** analysis of any stock.

The clearest and most important information you'll receive about Teeny Bopper stocks comes from the market. Iomega was still losing money long after it had double, tripled and quadrupled in price. But its new Zip drives were flying off the shelves. Informed investors knew that. They knew that big profits were just around the corner, and were pushing Iomega's price higher and higher. So if a Teeny Bopper's price keeps going higher and higher over a period of months, buy it even though the fundamentals have not yet materialized.

IV. MANAGING YOUR PORTFOLIO. Let there be no mistake, dealing with Teeny Boppers is a high risk investment strategy. One way to mitigate this risk is to spread your bets in equal dollar amounts over at least 10 stocks. With this many stocks, you can begin to tolerate the wild price swings that are normal for Teeny Boppers.

High volatility is the blessing and the curse of Teeny Boppers. You've got to be willing to accept rapid price swings of 20 to 30 percent, but you also need to know when to get out of a stock. Normally, one would exit a stock that drops 10 to 20 percent. I would suggest that you would change this guideline to 20 to 40 percent with Teeny Boppers. Even if you lost 40 percent on a single stock, it would be only four percent of a ten stock investment.

Keep plugging. You may find that many of your selections lose money. But don't get discouraged. One ten bagger will more than make up for a lot of little losses.

V. ALTERNATIVE METHODS. Even though it's a lot of fun to pick winners and make money at the same time, there are much easier ways to make money with Teeny Boppers. For example, I use VectorVest ProGraphics. It provides daily analyses of Value, Safety and Timing for over 7,600 stocks. Over 1,200 of these stocks are under $6.00, and many are traded on the NASDAQ Small Cap Exchange. VectorVest also provides Buy, Sell, Hold recommendations and Stop-Prices on every stock. This takes a lot of the guesswork out of owning Teeny Boppers. From January 6 through March 10, 1995, VectorVest Gave Iomega eleven consecutive Buy recommendations as it rose in prices from 4 3/8 to 7 3/8 (prior to splitting 3 for 1).

The number of winners VectorVest ProGraphics discovers is incredible. Our "Beeline Boppers" strategy which if fully documented gave an annualized return of 100.4%. It clearly shows that Teeny Boppers are the low-prices stocks with explosive price appreciation potential.

High Performers: Where Profits Reign Supreme

In the last chapter, I referred to a list of 50 stocks that I published on January 20, 1995 called "High Performers." You may recall that this list contained sensational winners such as US Robotics, Ascend Communications, and Iomega. This portfolio of stocks gained 20.3% from January 14, 1995 to April 14, 1995 for an annualized rate of 80.9%.

From January 14, 1995 to May 30, 1997, the 43 stocks still being traded gained an average of 173% for an annualized rate of 133.9%. Twenty two of the 50 stocks gained more than 100%, and only four of the 43 actively traded stocks are showing losses. How can you find these guys?

The key to selecting "High Performers" is to start with a list of stocks hitting new 52 week highs. Stocks hitting new highs are deviating from normal pricing behavior in a very special way, and deserve special attention. These stocks are identified in all the papers, so it's easy to begin your selection process. The hard part comes in shrinking this list to the most probable winners. Here's how to do it:

BUY STOCKS WITH THE BEST COMBINATIONS OF
VALUE, SAFETY AND TIMING

Every investor needs to know what stock is really worth, how safe it is, and when to buy, sell or hold. I like to buy safe, undervalued stocks that are rising in price. Sounds good, but let's examine these criteria more closely:

VALUATION: When the Price of a stock is less than or equal to its inherent value, you're buying stock in a company that is making money, and that's very important. In today's hyper-inflated market, hundreds of stocks are selling at ridiculously high P/E ratios, and they are bound to crash someday. Stocks of companies with solid earnings have a better chance of prevailing in good times and bad.

SAFETY: Stocks of companies with consistent, predictable financial performance are well managed and will outperform the market in the long-term. They are more likely to fulfill your expectations of earnings growth and price appreciation. That's what stock safety is all about.

GROWTH: Stocks with earnings growth rates above 12 percent per year are likely to demonstrate above average performance. Stocks with low earnings growth rates have little to look forward to, even if they have recently hit new highs. Safe, undervalued stocks with above average growth rates are the creme-de-la-creme. These stocks tend to make new highs year after year. What could be better than that?

PRICE PERFORMANCE: If you want to own stocks with rising prices, buy stocks with rising prices. This idea is very hard for many investors to accept, but the best thing that can happen to your portfolio is to own a group of stocks which are hitting new highs.

Screening your original list of stocks hitting new 52 week highs with these criteria will result in a "short-list" of final candidates for purchase. This would take a ton of work, and hours of time to do manually. Not to fear. VectorVest ProGraphics is here.

The list of "High Performers" cited at the beginning of this chapter was selected by VectorVest ProGraphics is less than 20 seconds. VectorVest ProGraphics searched over 7,600 stocks for stocks hitting new 52 week highs, and ranked them by VST-Vector, a proprietary indicator which I developed. My approach to assessing Value, Safety and Timing has been discussed in previous chapters of this book. I combine my proprietary indicators, RV, RS, and RT into a master indicator called VST-Vector.

Stocks with high VST-Vector values have the best combinations of Value, Safety, and Timing. They consistently outperform the market. Applying the power of VST-Vector analysis to stocks hitting new 52 week highs allows me to focus on the best performing stocks with the best fundamentals. It gives me a steady flow of High Performers: Where Profits Reign Supreme.

Super Star Stocks

What does it take to be a Super Star? Performance. Outstanding performance. Not for a day, a week, or even a year. It has to be done over a period of years.

Everyone knows that Michael Jordan, Joe Montana, and Jack Nicklaus were Super Stars. Their performances were visible, and well documented. They were outstanding for a long period of time. Keeping score in the world of sports is straightforward, but it's not so easy with stocks. There are no universally accepted standards for measuring stock performance. Even if there were, the criteria would be less certain. So how can we identify Super Star Stocks?

One might be tempted to use price performance as the only characteristic of a Super Star Stock. But I've seen too many miserable stocks get pushed up by hype and fluff to be impressed by price performance. So let's go behind the scenes and look at the bottom line.

In the world of business, making money is the key measure of performance. Making money is the difference between winning and losing, prospering or struggling, surviving or dying. But making money is not enough to spawn a Super Star. A company has to make more money quarter after quarter for a long time.

Companies which consistently generate higher and higher earnings at tremendous rates create Super Star Stocks.

It's terribly difficult to grow earnings at high rates over a period of years. It requires a rare combination of superb management, quality products, and exceptional services. Consider the following story.

I was peacefully working on a quiet Sunday morning in July 1989 when my computer was jolted by a tremendous surge of electricity. The picture on my monitor spiralled into a back hole. Everything stopped in an eerie silence. I sat there stunned and dumbfounded.

Of course, I was well aware of the damage a power surge could do to delicate electronic equipment. I had experienced the nuisance of power outages during storms, and typically unplugged my computer when I was away from home. Never, however, did I expect to be zapped on a clear, blue Sunday morning.

Fortunately, my surge protector sacrificed itself, and limited the damage to the computer. The hard drive survived, and so did I. But I learned a lesson. The next day I bought a tape back-up system, and an auxiliary power supply.

The manufacturer of the auxiliary power supply was American Power Conversion Incorporated, a young company with the right product at the right time. Did it have the management to become a success?

American Power Conversion (APC) was formed in 1985 and went public in 1988. Earnings turned positive after one year of operation, and increased at a tremendous rate. Its stock price soared, and the stock split five times. One hundred shares in 1988 became 3,200 shares by June 1995.

Skeptics abounded, and APC's stock became a favorite target of short-sellers. Could APC maintain its blistering pace of sales and earnings growth? Indeed it could. Sales rose from $17 million in 1988 to $413 million in 1996. Per share earnings rose from 5 cents per share in 1988 to 77 cents in 1994. Earnings increased for 25 consecutive quarters. APC consistently demonstrated outstanding performance. It was a Super Star Stock.

VectorVest defines a Super Star Stock as one having a Relative Safety rating of 1.20 or more, and a forecasted earnings growth rate of at least 20 percent per year. As of May 30, 1997, only 51 of over 6,000 stocks in our database met these requirements. Table I. shows 10 Super Star stocks ranked by Value-Safety-Timing Vector.

Table I. Selected Super Stocks (Ranked by VST-Vector)

Company Name	Price	RV	RS	RT	VST	GRT	REC
Gulf SoMedSup	19.8	1.51	1.39	1.42	1.44	+21	B
Fastenal Co.	46.8	1.22	1.47	1.41	1.38	+20	B
Dollar Genl	33.6	1.34	1.40	1.24	1.36	+21	B
Intel	151.5	1.61	1.40	1.11	1.36	+25	B
Cisco Systems	67.8	1.38	1.27	1.39	1.35	+27	B
Schwab, Chas.	40.6	1.21	1.22	1.51	1.34	+21	B
MBNA Corp.	33.9	1.42	1.41	1.16	1.32	+20	B
Oxford Hlth.	70.5	1.24	1.33	1.34	1.31	+22	B
Oracle Sys	46.6	1.28	1.39	1.22	1.29	+22	B
Robert Half	42.9	1.30	1.26	1.20	1.25	+25	B

Price = Closing Price as of 06/30/97.

RV = Relative Value*
RS = Relative Safety*
RT = Relative Timing*
VST = Value-Safety-Timing Vector*
GRT = Earnings Growth Rate in Percent Per Year
REC = Recommendation (B = Buy) *Values above 1.00 are Favorable

Each of the companies listed in Table I has strong upside price appreciation potential as reflected in the high RV values. They have extraordinary long-term records of financial performance as shown by the RS values above 1.20, and they are in strong upward price moves. Of course, they all have forecasted earnings growth rates of 20%/year or more. Because of their super performance, they are all rated a Buy. They are all Super Star Stocks.

The Election Cycle

Interest rates are the single most powerful factor affecting the stock market. As sure as the moon causes ocean tides to rise and fall, interest rates cause stock prices to do the same. Stock prices go up when interest rates go down, and fall when interest rates go up.

There is another powerful force, however, that comes along every four years that overrules interest rates. It's The Presidential Cycle. It doesn't matter whether interest rates are rising or falling, the stock market goes up during the last two years of a presidential administration.

This phenomenon is neither coincidental nor accidental. It is the result of political forces striving to boost the economy. A prosperous economy and a booming stock market virtually guarantee reelection of an incumbent administration.

According to Yale Hirsch, Editor of the 1997 Stock Trader's Almanac, "the last two years of the 41 administrations since 1832 produced a total net market gain of 592% compared with 79% gain of the first two years of these administrations. The average gains were 14.4% and 1.9% respectively.

Clearly, incumbent administrations not only strive to look good in the last two years in office, but they make the hard decisions, such as raising taxes, during the first two years.

The stock market rose 12% in 1992, the year Mr. Clinton was elected. It went up 7% in 1993, his first year in office, and fell 2 percent in 1994, his second year in office. The average gain for Mr. Clinton's first two years in office was 2.5%, not far from the historical average of 1.9%.

The stock market, as measured by the S&P 500 Index, was up a sensational 43.0% in the third year of Mr. Clinton's administration, and 22.9% in 1996. This performance was well above the historical average of 14.4% gain for the last two years in office. Does this mean the market will correct in 1997 and 1998?

Not necessarily, but there is very little chance that 1997 and 1998 also will be outstanding years for the market. It appears that 1997 will be an up year for the stock market, but it will likely fall short of the boomers we experienced in 1995 and 1996.

This observation is based upon a number of factors. First of all, it's a simple statistical phenomenon that large gains are followed by smaller gains and vice-versa. Since the 1995 and 1996 gains are large by most standards, the 1997-1998 gains are likely to be far less.

Another piece of evidence supporting this view is the observation made by Mr. Dick A. Stoken, in his book "Strategic Investment Timing." He states that, "The really juicy part of the election cycle is the fifteen-month period beginning in early October, two years before the election, and lasting until early January of the election year." In other words, the juicy part of this election cycle started early in October 1994 and ended early in January 1996.

Mr. Stoken justifies this claim by noting that from 1934 through 1982, the market gained an average of 25% during this fifteen month period compared to only 1% for the other 33 months of an administration's term in office. Since Mr. Stoken's book was published in 1984, I performed the same calculations for 1986, 1990, and 1994. The averages were as follows:

Election	Prime 15 Months % Gain/(Loss)	Other 33 Months Year % Gain/(Loss)
1982	38.0	44.5
1986	7.3	26.2
1990	24.5	26.7
1994	33.1	n/a

We see here that the presidential election cycles of 1982, 1986, and 1990 contradict Mr. Stoken's claim that the "Prime 15 months" outperform the "other 33 months." The last time this happened was in the period from 1942 through 1950. Subsequently, (from 1954 through 1978), the "Prime 15 Months" of The Presidential Cycle far outgained the "Other 33 Months." Is this about to happen again? History says it is.

While it's fun studying historical phenomenon such as The Presidential Cycle, one would be better served by staying with fundamentals. Stock prices rise when inflation and interest rates go down and earnings go up. This is exactly what happened in 1995 and 1996, but the trends are likely to weaken in 1997 and 1998. Inflation will not go down much further, so interest rates will have a bias to rise. Earnings growth is still on the rise, but the rate of earnings growth is slowing.

This scenario says that the stock market will be OK in 1997 and questionable in 1998. Obviously, we have seen the best of The Presidential Cycle. According to Mr. Stoken, the next big up-move in the market will begin in October 1998. Mark this date on your calendar.

Timing the Market:
A System that has Never Failed

Being on the wrong side of the market is the worst thing that can happen to an investor. It doesn't have to happen to you.

Old Joe Granville always said the market tells its own story. All you have to do is read what it is saying. Unfortunately for him, he didn't take his own advice.

Joe Granville was one of the pioneers of technical analysis. He used several novel methods of "reading the market." The most popular of which is On Balance Volume. Initially, he was quite successful, and became the market "Guru" of the early 1980's. He was so influential that his forecasts became self-fulfilling prophecies. Then he missed the call on the greatest Bull market of all time. On August 16, 1982, the market broke out of a steep slump, and Joe Granville said it was a folly. He said that it was a Bull trap, rising stock prices were like balloons that were about to burst. He remained a Bear for over 14 years while the market soared. What went wrong?

Mr. Granville's fatal error is that he went from timing the market to forecasting it. There is an enormous difference between the two. Market timers study indicators of market activity to determine whether it is rising or falling.

Forecasters consider economic factors, and whatever else they think is important to predict what the market will do. Market timers need never fail. All forecasters will fail eventually.

Forecasting the market is theoretically far more powerful than timing. Everyone would like to know what the market is going to do, when it will happen and by how much. In the real world, however, nobody has a crystal ball. Forecasting deals with the unknown, and eventual error is certain. The landscape is full of forecasters who have gone wrong. Their stories are well documented, and they were viewed as stars when they were right. Now they are viewed as losers. Joe Granville? He just happened to be the most flamboyant of the bunch. Recently, he too has turned Bullish. Maybe that's something to worry about.

This chapter is not about forecasting the market. It's about timing, i.e., reading our indicators and letting them tell us when the market is rising or falling. It's about sensing turning points and knowing when to invest aggressively, and when to take defensive actions. We want to buy within five percent of a bottom and sell within five percent of a top. Can we do it? It's really very simple.

The market timing system described below depends upon two key indicators:

1. The Price of the VectorVest Composite, and

2. The VectorVest Recommendation Profile.

Both indicators were developed by VectorVest, a stock analysis system which analyzes over 7,600 stocks each day for Value, Safety and Timing, and gives Buy, Sell, Hold recommendations on each stock each day.

The Price of the VectorVest Composite is the most important indicator used in timing the market. This indicator is the average price of all the stocks in the VectorVest database. It is reported each week in VectorVest Views, a commentary on the market, along with Stop-Price and Relative Timing in the following manner: VectorVest Composite, (04/11/97).

Param.	03/07	03/14	03/21	03/27	04/04	04/11
Price	21.4	21.1	20.6	20.4	19.9	19.7
Stop	20.2	20.2	19.9	19.7	19.5	19.3
RT	0.95	0.95	0.85	0.83	0.75	0.80

Price = Average Price of all stocks in VV database
Stop = Average Stop-Price of all stocks
RT   = Average Relative Timing of all stocks

When the Price of the VectorVest Composite is moving in a given direction, the market is moving in the same direction. As shown above, the Price of the VectorVest Composite fell each week from 03/07/97 through 04/11/97. Therefore, the market was moving down during this period.

The VectorVest Recommendation Profile is the second important indicator used in timing the market. It gives the percentage of Buy, Sell, Hold recommendations in the VectorVest database each day. It is reported in VectorVest Views each week in the following manner: VVREC Profile of 5,860 Stocks in Percent (04/11/97).

REC	03/07	03/14	03/21	03/27	04/04	04/11
Buy	19.2	12.5	8.8	7.0	5.0	5.3
Hold	56.8	58.1	54.6	55.9	52.2	53.3
Sell	24.0	29.4	36.6	37.1	42.8	41.4
Total	100.0	100.0	100.0	100.0	100.0	100.0

When the ratio of Buys to Sells is above 1.00, the market is robust. Correspondingly, the market is weak when the Buy to Sell ratio is below 1.00. As you can see from the above data, the Buy to Sell ration was below 1.00 on 03/07/97 and continued to deteriorate through 04/04/97. This confirmed that the market was in a correction.

Those of you with good eyes may have noticed that RT, VectorVest's Relative Timing indicator, ticked upward on 04/11/97 even though the price of the VectorVest Composite went down. RT was sensing a change in momentum of the downward move. Sure enough, the market bottomed two weeks later.

A careful look at the Recommendation Profile shows that on 04/11/97 the percentage Buys increased and the percentage of Sells decreased from the prior week. This was another sign that the correction was nearing completion.

From the very beginning, (1988), we recognized that the VectorVest Recommendation Profile provided a measure of the pulse of the market. And it was used to help guide our thoughts on the direction of the market. But it was not until March of 1995, that we discovered how the Price of the VVC clearly signaled the direction of the market. We examined our data back to April 1991 (the time when we first began computing the VVC), and found that tracking the direction of the market with the Price of the VectorVest Composite was incredibly simple and reliable.

Here's how the system works. If the Price of the VectorVest Composite moves in a given direction two weeks without an intermediate contrary move, it gives a preliminary signal of the market's direction. If the preliminary signal is followed by another move in the same direction, the preliminary signal is reinforced, but not confirmed. We must turn to the VectorVest Recommendation Profile for confirmation of the market's direction.

In the data sets shown above you saw that the Price of the VectorVest Composite had been undergoing a steady week-to-week decline, and the ratio of Buys to Sells in the Recommendation Profile was well below 1.00. There was no question that the market was going down. Yet many analysts didn't realize this was happening. The Price of the VectorVest Composite peaked on February 14, 1997, (this is called a Turning Point), and gave a "DOWN" signal two weeks later on 02/28/97. The Price of the VectorVest Composite finally bottomed 10 weeks later on 04/25/97, 11.0 percent below the price reached on 02/14/97. (You may see this data in the VectorVest ProGraphics documentation.)

Although, we had discovered this timing technique in March 1995, the first major DOWN signal given in "real time" did not occur until 09/22/95. The market had just completed a marvelous Bull run lasting 39 weeks. Signs of weakness had begun to appear in July, but the market did not peak until 09/08/95. Two weeks later we got the DOWN signal. Here's what we said on 09/22/97: "The Price of our VectorVest Composite has now gone down for the second week without an intermediate upmove. Our studies have shown that this event signals a market correction. The still favorable investment climate suggests, however, that it will be only a mild correction. It's OK for Aggressive investors to buy high VST-Vector, "B" rated stocks, but Prudent investors should stand aside."

From September 22nd on, we tracked the correction week-by-week until it bottomed on January 12, 1996. Two weeks later, we said, "The Price of our Vector-Vest Composite rose for the second week in a row, signaling that the market's correction is over. Although the green light has not been confirmed by our Recommendation Profile, it's OK to buy high VST-Vector "B" rated stocks. It's a good time to go Bottom-Fishing. For a FREE copy of our Special Report **"Bottom-Fishing: The Art of Buying Low and Selling High,"** call 1-330-668-2814.

This downturn lasted 18 weeks and the Price of the VectorVest Composite fell 9.6 percent. This was the so called "Stealth Correction." Small-capitalization and NASDAQ stocks were getting hammered while the mighty Dow Jones Industrial Average was just doing fine, rising 8.9%. This deviation between the blue chip stocks and the rest of the market was just a forerunner of what was to happen for the next 18 months.

And so it has gone from Turning Point to Turning Point, from UP signal to DOWN signal, monitoring the market week after week, never missing a major move.

As of the current time, July 18, 1997, the market completed its 12th week of an UP move from a bottom reached on 04/25/97. When will this UP move end? We don't know. How high will it go? We don't know. But we will know when it ends, and when the next DOWN move has begun. At that time we'll be ready to use Stops, buy Puts, and Sell-Short.

You might believe that the market moves in a random fashion. It does not. While there are periods where the market moves up and down from week to week, it always happens within the framework of an underlying trend. The Price of the VectorVest Composite has reversed itself by going down two consecutive weeks and immediately turning up for two straight weeks only three times in more than six years. Only once, in 1994, has the Price of the VectorVest Composite moved up for two weeks, and then reversed into a downturn. These reversals happened within a flat or "trading range" market. In no case were major moves involved.

This system of timing the market has never failed to signal a major move...and it never will. The reason is quite simple. Big moves start with little moves. Even the apparently abrupt crash of October 1987 occurred nearly two months after the market peaked in late August 1987. Since we keep track of every little move the market makes, we will never miss a big move. What more could you ask for?

The drama of the market's moves is vividly displayed by VectorVest ProGraphics stock analysis and graphics software. You may call 1-888-658-7638 for a 5 Week Special Trial Offer of VectorVest ProGraphics. You'll receive 2 years of weekly data, 6 months of daily data on over 7,600 stocks, industry groups and sectors, a Users Guide & FREE instructional DVD FREE technical support and 5 weeks of Daily Updates for $9.95, a $20.00 savings from the regular price.

Knowledgeable Investors

Knowledge is power. Power is the ability to get things done. Knowledgeable investors have the power to pick the right stocks, know when to buy, sell or hold, and manage their portfolios for persistent profits.

Knowledge comes from experience and information. Experience cannot be purchased. There's a price to pay for experience, however, and it does not come cheaply. The price we pay is time, and the agony of learning from our failures. Experience comes only from one's personal involvement.

Information, on the other hand, can be purchased. It comes from others. Herein lies a problem. What we take as information may or may not be valid. Information is often misrepresented. Investors are often fooled into thinking they have purchased information when they actually have purchased data. Data and information are distinctly different. Data is a commodity, a mute documentation of the past. Information is a value added product. It speaks the future.

Information comes from the analysis of data, and is not better than the data and analysis from which it came. A thousand investors may read the same annual report. Each will analyze the report, and draw a different view of company's prospects. Those with greater experience, special skills or training are more likely to be right. The others are more likely to be wrong.

Investors are starved for information. They read books, magazines and newspapers, watch TV, attend seminars, and belong to investor groups to learn as much as they can. It seems that the world is awash in information. But good information is hard to find.

Knowledgeable investors know that information is unlikely to be reliable unless the cause and effect relationships within the data have been tested and verified. Statistical analysis is a powerful tool for analyzing data. But it's not the only one. Common sense is your most important asset.

Most of what we receive as information is not reliable. This so called "information" is flawed either by improper or insufficient analysis, or by deliberate design to get your hard earned dollars. Buyer beware holds especially true in the financial markets.

In selecting stocks, your primary job is that of assessing information. Many investors, however, feel qualified and prefer to analyze data. This is fine as long as they have the time, resources and skills to produce reliable results. Knowledgeable investors can save time, and get excellent results by asking the right questions. Can you answer the following questions for the stocks in your portfolio?

* Is the company making money?
* What is the stock really worth?
* Is the stock over or undervalued?
* How safe is the stock?
* Is its price rising or falling?
* What is its forecasted earnings per share?
* What is its estimated earnings growth rate?
* What is its growth to P/E ratio?
* What are its dividends per share?
* How safe are the dividends?
* How fast are dividends growing?
* Does this stock meet my risk/reward objectives?
* Should I buy it now?
* When should I sell it?

VectorVest ProGraphics answers all these questions systematically, objectively and unemotionally. Compare these answers with those of other reliable sources. It's the right thing to do. Using VectorVest with other sources gives you more power to pick the right stocks, and make the right decision. This will help you manage your portfolio for persistent profits. When you combine experience with good information, you'll have what it takes to join that elite class of Knowledgeable Investors.